RED
PONCHO
and
BIG BOOTS

RED
PONCHO
and
BIG BOOTS

The Life of Murray Dickson

JIM PALMER

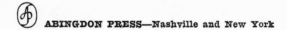

ABINGDON PRESS—Nashville and New York

RED PONCHO AND BIG BOOTS

Copyright © 1969 by Abingdon Press

Standard Book Number: 687-35879-5
Library of Congress Catalog Card Number: 70-84715

SET UP, PRINTED AND BOUND BY THE
PARTHENON PRESS, AT NASHVILLE,
TENNESSEE, UNITED STATES OF AMERICA

To Murray's Nova
without whom Murray could not have lived the story
and
To My Ellen
without whom I could not have written the story

FOREWORD

History is essentially the impact of personalities and not simply a series of circumstances or events. This book is the story of the life of a man who rightfully could be called a molder of circumstances and a creator of events. His imprint and contribution to the development of the church in Bolivia lead us to add his name to that great list of others who through the years have stood out among their brethren as men of courage and vision.

The impact of his contributions has been enlarged by pastors and congregations in the United States who joined together to carry out "Operation Murray Dickson." This proved to be the actualization of the ideals for which he stood, and took the form of: providing the means to broaden the services being offered by the church, establishing new and creative forms of ministry, and providing the resources for the development and training of leaders. It proved to be the continuance of the impact of his personality.

Those who came in contact with him found one whose life was ablaze with a cause which, in turn, came to be a source of inspiration and commitment in their own lives. Yet one was never left in doubt concerning what this cause was which motivated him. His life was always pointing beyond himself to another. And therefore this is not simply a story of a man's life, but rather of a cause which consumed his life to the last.

In this sense it is everyman's story, and we trust by retelling it shall be a source of inspiration to us all.

Paul McCleary
Executive Secretary
The Methodist Church in Bolivia

PREFACE

This story had to be written. All the excuses I could muster couldn't put out of my mind the compulsion to write, however inadequate, a historical record of one to whom I owe so much.

Just as all who came in touch with Murray Dickson, I was immediately made a follower and captivated admirer. Even in his death I found spiritual depths that I never dreamed of.

To pay adequate tribute while being objectively accurate is an impossible task. Yet it had to be done, and for seven years I struggled to produce a story which would portray the spirit of the man. It is the story of hard work and dedication.

For assistance in preparation I am deeply indebted to Murray's parents, Mr. and Mrs. George Dickson, who shared Murray's correspondence from the day he left for Southern Methodist University. One stinging regret is that I did not complete the manuscript before "Dad George" passed away. I trust that "Mama Jennie" will find such pride in it as to somewhat remedy my tardiness.

Murray's wife, Nova, gave unstintingly of her time and recollection of events and persons. His children added their comments and read the materials faithfully. My wife added the necessary encouragement and provided quiet times for writing and rewriting, as did my children. My congregation provided certain freedom to permit the detailed research and writing periods as well as travel. To all those who assisted in typing and other chores, I am forever grateful.

I must acknowledge the unnumbered persons who, from Murray's days at S.M.U. and on furloughs and his early days in Bolivia, added those little personal touches to make the book readable as well as accurate.

A deep personal debt must be acknowledged to Bishop Sante Uberto Barbieri, one of the real saints of the twentieth century Christian church. His assistance was invaluable and highly appreciated. His own book *El Sacrificio Vivo* (*The Sacrificial Life*) reaches the spiritual heights I wish I might have been able to accomplish.

PREFACE

My prayer is that through this volume, the missions of the church may become a reality and a personal concern. In a person such as Murray Dickson, the grace of God comes alive and must continue to work its miracles.

Jim Palmer
Plano, Texas

CONTENTS

RED PONCHO AND BIG BOOTS

THE MAN
with the
BIG FEET

The morning was warm and sunny. The sky was a brilliant blue as can be found only in a spot with the rarefied air of the Bolivian capital, located at 13,000 feet above sea level. My thoughts were miles away as I sat in the chair provided by the chubby, one-legged shoeshine boy. Pursuing the latest news and pondering Spanish words which taxed my vocabulary, I was lost in concentration.

A tug on my pants leg distracted me, and I looked down into the big eyes of the Aymara Indian who was working at the high gloss he loved to put on the toes of my shoes. Then, in one of his rare attempts at conversation, he asked, "Where is the man with the big feet?"

Not tumbling immediately to his reference, I must have looked a little puzzled as he reached deep into his kit of various polishes. It was then I realized that he

15

was referring to Murray Dickson. Who else would have provided a poor, illiterate shoeshine boy with special polish to enable him to take pride in a special shine for cordovan shoes?

The events of the nightmarish tragedy five months earlier raced across my mind. Surely someone had told this boy about the accident high in the Bolivian Andes in which two Methodist missionaries had died. Still, who would know of his interest in the man whose shoes he shined so regularly during previous years?

Slowly, in halting Spanish, I attempted to tell of the tragedy. As I finished, big tears began to stream across the bronzed cheeks and drop on my shoes. Then, with a look of reverence and awe I had never beheld before, stumbling words spoken in anguished sincerity gushed forth: "He was a good friend! He was a good pastor and teacher! He was a man with great sympathy for the problems of the Bolivian people! He was a Christian gentleman!"

There was no mistaking the intent of this humble and heart-stirring praise; the shoeshine boy had lost a friend. Only later would I learn of the love and affection which had grown between this illiterate amputee and one of the servants of God whose influence was welcomed in the most important offices and most humble homes throughout his adopted country of Bolivia.

THE MAN WITH THE BIG FEET

As I got up to leave, the shoeshine boy was packing his little kit of brushes and polishes. As we parted, both deeply moved, I realized that this boy, one of the most common of the common, was too moved by the loss of a friend to continue with the day's work. I last saw him that day with his kit over his shoulder, crutch in one hand and customer's chair in the other, heading up the street toward his home.

In successive visits to have my shoes shined before visiting in town, the story unfolded. Murray had provided a friendship which was lasting. He conversed with the boy; he secured medicine and medical aid for the family at a local Methodist hospital; he never gave less than twenty times the usual price for a shine and seldom missed a generous tip. All these gestures won a friend who would remember him, not by name, but would describe him as so many knew him—the man with the big feet.

This is Murray's story, told as I observed it and heard versions related by those who lived it with one who personified his Master.

THE
PROCESS
BEGINS

The home was humble, the fare common to farm tables of north Texas cotton land. A wholesome pride instilled in each member of the family made every meal or time of fellowship something to be savored and held dear.

Natural thrift was a part of the heritage Murray received from Jennie and George Dickson as their life revolved around typical farming activities of the late 1920's. George Dickson loved the soil; young Murray was carefully instructed in soil conservation and use. In later years Murray described soil, plants, and crops he had observed while traveling.

Infrequent letters in later years portrayed living conditions of the people he met in his travels. One such letter, written in a schoolboy's notebook, covered the entire eighty-one bound pages. In contrast to his father's firm, beautiful hand, Murray's writing was often a scribble which took an experienced eye to decipher. When forced to write, he apologized for not having inherited his father's talents in penmanship.

Murray's early days were filled with physical labor. In mature years he habitually returned to some form of physical exertion to "work the kinks out of my body." Long walks and yard and gardening work always restored his sense of humor and perspective. He delighted in reporting such diversions to his father to prove he remembered his background. Sights, sounds, and smells were deeply ingrained in the youth.

On a crisp, frosty morning in November shortly after beginning his study at Southern Methodist University, he reported to his father in a letter, "As I walked out the front door of Dallas Hall . . . and a breath of cold air with just a suspicion of a smell of wood smoke caught me, it brought back vividly the thought: this is hog-killin' weather." Such an appreciation for rural life enabled Murray to establish a rapport with the poverty-stricken farmers of Bolivia and other countries where he traveled.

Murray seldom missed nature's tender beauty in a flower, often carefully preserving one to present to his wife at the end of an extended trip into the country.

Not all was smooth for the growing Murray. Through a series of object lessons his grandmother, Mamma

May, who lived with the family, taught him to control a hot, quick temper. His grandmother's admonitions nurtured a keenly sensitive spirit, which became a great asset in the years of trial in difficult situations where men familiar with every means of deceit and provocation tested his patience.

Along with a love of things basic to farming, Murray exhibited a great thirst for knowledge, which the family recognized. They helped him cultivate his mind and provided opportunities to acquire further training. Years after he had chopped his last row of cotton, he was keenly alert to cotton prices and the political tides affecting farming. When debating in college he was quick to select questions pertaining to agriculture as areas of contest.

The logical mind entered its agile years while Murray attended Hillsboro Junior College. There he excelled in debating and edited the college newspaper during the 1933-34 school year. His debating skill won him a reputation and a number of honors in intersectional contests.

God, the family, and the farm were the major concerns in Murray's early life. He joined the Methodist Episcopal Church, South, in 1924. His orientation to the church, college, and future was influenced by the wholesome home and the two strong, but very different, personalities of his parents.

A gentle concern for his parents and his love for them permeated all his communications. Murray seldom missed recognizing a birthday, Mother's or Father's Day, or an anniversary. His tributes to his parents were filled with devotion and a growing concern for their health as the years passed. The few visits he made to his parents were occasions for wringing the last possible ounce of sweetness and satisfaction from the relationship between mother, father, and son.

Completing his study at Hillsboro Junior College, Murray entered Southern Methodist University in the fall of 1934. Soon afterward he numbered among his friends men who were destined for positions of distinguished leadership throughout the southwestern United States. Many of these would influence the life of the church when Murray offered their churches a vital message from the field of world missions.

Applying himself academically, Murray assured his parents, "I don't think you will get any deficiency reports."

Once established on campus, Murray sought to share in youth programs at church. In a matter of weeks he was called on to substitute as teacher for adult classes, some of which later paid him a handsome five dollars per Sunday. By his own admissions he gave a decidedly political science flavor to the presentation of the gospel as he taught and interpreted it.

Money was a concern. Descriptions of his daily meals reassured his parents who were concerned about his eating habits. By eating in his room, he saved one half the cost of breakfast. He often waited tables in a fraternity house for a free lunch and ate sparingly at a cafeteria for the evening meal. In his senior year at S.M.U., Murray wrote, "I am staying at a lovely place about three blocks from the university in the home of Dr. Glanville. My roommate is Bill Dickinson, a splendid fellow in his first year in the School of Theology. The room costs me $8.50 per month with linens and towels furnished and laundered."

Using typical college-boy psychology on his mother in reports of room and board, Murray would mention a special kind of cookie for which he was hungry. Mamma Jennie, well known for her cooking and baking, almost always complied with a big box of homemade cookies and goodies. The post-depression years were difficult, and the letters home were filled with comments to convince the family he was economizing.

Student work and interests called for increased travel. Dr. L. F. Sensabaugh, teacher in Christian education at the School of Theology and staff member at

Highland Park Methodist Church, offered Murray considerable encouragement as he assumed more leadership. At one point, when his finances became more strained than usual, Murray refused to attend a student conference. Asked by Dr. Sensabaugh why, Murray replied with the frank admission, "Simply this, Doctor. Everywhere I've gone the last two years I've gone on charity. I'm sick and tired of it, and I'm not going anywhere again until I can pay for it out of my own pocket!"

The outcome was that Dr. Sensabaugh paid the registration and arranged for Murray to drive a car and lead the S.M.U. delegation. Murray never forgot the argument that there was a need for his ability while others had the resources.

As he faced decisions about his future, new faces and new ideas confronted him. Clark Eichelberger of the American League of Nations Association offered him a position with that group. Murray described him as a "splendid fellow, even though a Yankee."

Then big business intervened. Hearing of the need for lecturers at the 1936 Texas Centennial Exhibition, Murray applied for a job. His talents and appearance were rewarded with one of the top-paying jobs in the General Motors auditorium, where for the rest of the summer he stood in the display hall and gave a flowery fifteen-minute pitch about the 1936 Chevrolet Master Deluxe.

Permanent offers of employment reached him from schools. He politely turned down contracts to teach in Frisco and Trinidad, Texas, at salaries of $95 and $120 per month, respectively. The summer helped Murray make up his mind. He would seek a master's degree in political science and take advantage of a teaching fellowship offered by S.M.U.

With pride in the fact of being at least partially self-supporting, Murray began his first year of teaching and study in graduate school. Assistance from a family estate had provided Murray with the opportunity for advanced education. He was always conscious of his responsibility to the family and considered the loan a sacred trust.

Some of the indebtedness Murray felt was to his uncle, Dwight Simmons, a well-established and highly respected Dallas lawyer. A mutual respect kept uncle and nephew in close communication during Murray's university years. Though frequent visits demonstrated their opposed political views, they spent hours in friendly debate. In later years Uncle Dwight, as an influential member of Highland Park Methodist Church, came to be a very generous supporter of Murray's work.

A STRUGGLE
TOWARD
DECISION

Murray came quickly to love the classroom where minds were molded. He accelerated his own academic pursuits and began correspondence with schools where he might complete a doctorate in political science. Church, classroom, and study carrel occupied most of his time. His social life was erratic. He offered the opinion to his father that dating was a waste of time with so many important things to be done. Several young ladies did receive a qualified kind of attention until lack of money or conflict of ideals led Murray to dismiss them as serious objects of his attention.

A quiet but insistent voice began to sound in Murray's life in the spring of 1937. He casually mentioned that he would be going to Greenville to "preach." This was different from the Sunday school classes he was teaching. He was quietly humble about taking the gospel in his hands and delivering it; still he began to fill small church pulpits in the Dallas area.

The second year in graduate school proved more complicated. Changes in faculty provided an opportunity for Murray to teach more advanced courses, with the provision that he continue toward the completion of his master's thesis that school year. A class in European government emphasized for him the crisis in the scene where dictatorships threatened peace. The teachings of his home came to the fore and the solid philosophy of individual integrity shone through Murray's ever-more-polished personality.

Working with Dr. Meyers of S.M.U. in preparing for the Institute of Public Affairs convention at Mexico City, Murray met dignitaries from all over the world. These contacts were to play an important role in his life before he knew it.

After innumerable corrections Murray completed and submitted his thesis as one in which he could take pride as "readable, not just scholarly." The subject was "Reorganization of the Texas Legislature."

Just before graduation ceremonies Murray accounted for the long list of friends he had made at S.M.U. In the roll call he mentioned: Morris Keeton, who would complete his Ph.D. and return to S.M.U. to teach, Finis Crutchfield studying at Duke, Sterling Wheeler at Union Theological Seminary, and Ewart Watts at Yale —all ministerial students and close friends. In commenting on their scattered circumstances, Murray observed, "The old gang is pretty well scattered. I had a chance to go to Union on a fellowship and with a job to pay all expenses, but *I just didn't feel that I was cut out to be a minister, so I turned it down.*"

With an eye on the address he was to deliver at the Hillsboro Junior College homecoming, Murray received his Master of Arts degree in political science at S.M.U. in ceremonies in late May.

One final task in connection with S.M.U. remained to be fulfilled in the summer of 1938. An unexplained attraction drew Murray to Mt. Sequoyah at Fayetteville, Arkansas, for the Young People's Leadership Conference of the southern Methodist Church. Going only as an observer, he was nevertheless elected president of the group and directed to attend the National Council of Methodist Youth of the northern Methodist Church, which met later in the summer in Colorado. Four hundred youth thrust leadership upon the shoulders of one whose spirit was more obvious to those around him than to Murray himself. That election placed him on the ground floor of youth activities at the time when the three segments of The Methodist Church were preparing for union.

The climax to his summer of student work and exposure to leadership was an invitation from the Wesley Foundation at Austin, Texas, to assume a position as student worker there. Many had recognized in Murray the qualities they sought; conversations between the Rev. Horace M. King and Dr. Sensabaugh had resulted in the formal invitation.

As he did in all decisions, Murray weighed the pros and cons. Something had happened to him during that summer which he could not explain. He recognized that the setting in Austin would permit him the opportunity of observing the state political arena first-hand, as well as give him a chance to pursue a doctorate and enjoy the cultural climate.

A continuing refrain had begun to run through Murray's mind: "Here is a chance to do something significant." In the final analysis he admitted his love for people and his desire to serve them. He accepted the position and began his work in September, 1938.

The teacher had become a pastor! Working under the direction of Dr. C. W. Hall and Dr. Edmund Heinsohn, Murray found that campus life suited him. Stirring young minds with the solid concepts of Christian and democratic thinking became his passion.

The new position was the most widely diversified experience he had ever known. He was administrator, but also pastor. It took all his ingenuity to help a vast number of students struggling with their personal problems and still keep them within the influence of the church.

Developing leadership in the foundation was a new problem. He could not reach down into each life and mold it to his thinking. Neither could he always accept the suggestions and directions the students wished to take. He was frustrated at times because of failures of students who should have been top leaders. Thus he learned a most important lesson and a recurring theme in his life: when he had done his best with all the inadequacies of human beings, he would pray and then leave the rest to God.

Murray was stimulated by discovering the potential for education in the discussion method. Small discussion groups multiplied as he found this method would offer persons the opportunity to express ideas and refine concepts while they were exposed to discussion.

One such attempt at the informal exchange of ideas produced "The Cosmopolitan Club." Supposedly based on international and more sophisticated concepts, it never rose to the heights Murray had envisioned. Watching from his position as director, Dr. Hall was not too surprised when Murray showed up one morning with the candidly humorous observation, "That brainchild of mine is an idiot!" The club promptly disbanded.

Church people were relieved to find such a candid voice in their student center at the state capital. At the same time they were completely taken with Murray's winsome manner and diplomatic handling of touchy subjects. People felt that he was a man of integrity to whom they could entrust their sons—and more, with whom they could trust their daughters.

Murray took advantage of every opportunity to travel and learn student work. In every conference and meeting he made lasting impressions because of his questions and observations.

As world conditions grew ominous, Murray was obsessed with two major concerns. One was the unexplained concern he felt toward the ministry of the church. The other was his deeply embedded convictions about war and the need for peace.

In searching for answers, Murray returned to the wisdom of his father. These views were suddenly beginning to be very important. Watching the political machinery of the state from close quarters caused Murray to revise some of his concepts of government. He woke to the deeper meaning of social responsibility for the individual citizen.

The spring of 1939 saw Murray teaching a full schedule, replacing Dr. Hall, who was ill. Again the excitement of the classroom stimulated him, but he bemoaned the limited time available for preparation. For the first time he taught a course in which he was forced to rely on the experiences of other people. The lectures on family relations were new to him, and he followed the advice of Dr. Hall and his notes carefully.

An increased schedule was complicated by time spent in planning a summer of traveling and leading student conferences. Time seemed so important. He detested wasting even a minute, as was illustrated in a note to his parents which began with the curt heading: "Aboard . . . special wreck, sitting in the station . . . wishing the thing would move out or that they would tell us how much longer overtime it is going to be."

Not all Murray's impatience was so expressed. Periodically his accumulated frustrations would be released through some cryptic statement to understanding friends, if they were nearby, or in a note like that quoted above. He seldom, if ever, allowed his frustrations to offend those who were responsible for the delays and frustrations.

One of the first responsibilities awaiting Murray upon return to Austin in the fall was to preach for Dr. Heinsohn. It was another step nearer the goal he could not see. He held no fear, but documented his sermons with background materials from the political situation as he spoke out against everything he felt negated the cause of Jesus Christ. It was evident that he was a pacifist. Dr. Heinsohn remembered, "Murray was little disturbed by thought of the consequences when he was sure he was right."

Famous personalities crossed Murray's path regularly. Harold Fey of the Fellowship of Reconciliation, Muriel Lester, the famous Englishwoman lecturer, and many other personalities influenced Murray as he sought to provide students with thinking other than the blind, patriotic cheers being raised on campuses.

To expose the students to these outstanding minds, lecture series were highlights during the year. One lecturer was a noted Negro educator, Dean Faulkner of Fisk University. During the time he was on campus, Dean Faulkner assisted Dr. Hall and Dr. Heinsohn in serving Holy Communion in University Methodist Church of Austin. It was the first time a Negro had served the sacrament in that church, and the result was an immediate uproar. Even those who were not at the service joined in the call for an investigation.

Among those asked to the hearing was Murray. When his time came to make a statement, he was firm but polite in saying that Dean Faulkner had made a marvelous contribution through his lectures and that he had been proud to receive Communion from him.

A woman rose and addressed Murray. "Mr. Dickson,

you have enjoyed the hospitality of our home, and you have eaten with us at times. You know how we love our Negro maid, but we wouldn't think of asking her to eat with us."

As she was speaking, Murray had assumed the manner familiar to those who knew him well. With his head tilted and his eyes looking slightly up and far away, he waited until the woman paused to consider her next words. He then responded quickly, "No ma'am, but I doubt that we would invite your Negro maid to lecture at the Wesley Foundation." The subtle humor, yet obvious truth of Murray's statement was reason to dismiss him from further questioning.

Murray spent the Christmas vacation of 1939 in Toronto, Canada, at a student congress. Leaders from the church in Europe moved Murray as they spoke. As he listened, his objections to world missions crumbled. Commenting on one of the leaders, Murray wrote, "Seeing him broken by the loss of his people makes war seem very real."

After hearing students take exact and articulate stands on issues confronting the world, Murray wrote that he felt that for the first time in his life he had observed Christian heroism. Doubtless some of that influence of deep conviction was stored in his own conscience for the time when he would face difficult decisions about his own involvement in war.

Returning to Austin, he found more and more preaching thrust upon him. Commenting on these pulpit appearances, Murray stated plainly to his mother, "This Sunday night I also preach at First Methodist Church . . . in place of a sick minister. I enjoy these contacts, but I like my work with students better."

Murray's sense of Christian responsibility was weighing heavily on a conscience that faced impending registration for the draft. He wrote his father, "I think now . . . more than ever, Christians need to learn to love and hope and pray, to keep their hearts clean of hatred and fear, to know that God's kingdom is not a visionary dream, but an attainable reality. . . . At any rate, in spite of the immediate cost of the thing, I know there will come an ultimate triumph of good; and my faith and confidence continue to increase."

October 16, 1940, was the date toward which Murray struggled with heavy heart. His mind kept turning back to the day when his father, perhaps blindly but in conviction objecting to the Boy Scout program as being militarily orientated, agreed to let Murray become a scout only if he would take an oath never to willingly bear arms against a fellowman.

The day before he registered for the draft, Murray

wrote his parents, "I feel I shall be compelled to register as a conscientious objector. My decision is not blind or anything. I know that I will be misunderstood by a great many people, including some I consider my best friends. Yet, I feel quite sure this is the only thing I can do in this case, and believing that, I shall have to stick to it."

It had been no shallow conflict of concerns. The probe of conscience had been thorough. Weighing the consequences and alternatives from every angle, Murray allowed no easy rationalization to compromise his conscience. He discussed these far-reaching implications with his students while at the same time insisting that they think for themselves and not be unduly swayed by his opinions.

Plaguing Murray as deeply as objecting to military service was the haunting fear that his time spent as an objector in conscience would be wasted. Rumors and unreliable reports had reached him that conscientious objectors were involved in various menial tasks which contributed nothing to humanity. Murray was convinced that such a waste of manly creativity was as much a sin as if he were to bear arms.

Compounding the difficulty of decision were the offers of various scholarships. Two of these were for study in schools of theology, which carried almost automatic deferment from service.

The registration was filed at the appointed time. One can read the existing carbon with the feeling that he can chart the development of a spirit through Murray's references, persons who had contributed influentially to his life. His travels had placed Murray in outstanding company within the church; he reflected this influence.

No sooner had the registration been filed than a further complication arose. Attending another student conference in late December, Murray was greeted by the congratulations of those who knew that he had been elected to represent the Methodist Student Movement at the International Congress of Students in Lima, Peru, in early 1941. At this news Murray's confusion was almost overwhelming.

A TRIP
TOWARD
DECISION

Previous travel had broadened Murray's horizons, but this trip opened a new world. From a conservative background with a tendency toward isolation, he was launched into an experience in which world missions of the church would become very personal.

As a fraternal delegate to the first Latin American Evangelical Youth Congress, he was given more than the usual duties. Instructed to get pictures and provided with camera and hard-to-get film, Murray sought to fulfill those requests from the Methodist Board of Missions. Friends urged him to extend the trip as far and as long as possible.

Shipboard talk with refugees fleeing the horrors of European persecutions, along with the earnest and eager Latin American youth, exposed Murray to totally new ideas. Such exposure was destined to change the course of his life. He mentioned the possibility of a trip to Bolivia in one letter to his parents.

Detailed descriptions of the people and the places where he saw deprivation overshadowed his reports of the conference. Murray's idealistic views were confronted by a continent ravaged by four centuries of colonial philosophy and exploitation which had been condoned by the Roman Catholic Church. Inclined to question the accusations made so blatantly by those who condemned Catholicism, Murray revised his ideas after observing the apparent lack of influence of the church in people's lives.

Noting the feverish pitch and exaggerated show of preparedness as they passed through the Panama Canal sent cold chills of apprehension up and down Murray's spine. He asked, "Could all this energy and motion and obvious force only be used and marshaled for the horrors of war?"

Very little effort was required on the part of Carlos Villapando, a Bolivian youth, and Mrs. Frank Beck to persuade him to extend his trip to Bolivia. Delayed on that trip in Arequipa, Peru, while awaiting the irregular overland transportation, Murray became well acquainted with a cultured Austrian woman whose story of being reduced from wealth, prestige, and culture to managing the hotel where he stayed duly impressed Murray.

When he arrived in La Paz after the rough trip

through the Andes, he discovered the Bolivians in the midst of the gala celebration of Carnaval. Since this is the period before Lent, all possible revelry is packed into three days and nights of drinking, dancing, and eating, mostly in that order. This colorful introduction to the people of Bolivia made a lasting impression on Murray.

In La Paz, Murray was entertained and escorted by Dr. and Mrs. Frank S. Beck. Along with his traveling companion, Tom Cromwell, Murray realized that the largest part of Methodist missions was educational. The teacher in him responded. Without his knowing it a plan was developing into a conviction and decision.

Ostensibly only fulfilling his interests as a tourist, Murray's mind was filling with unforgettable pictures. His mind returned to these and especially to the scene in Huancayo, Peru, where he and Tom had been with John Chappel, the young missionary who felt compelled to go to the desolate and hopeless little community of adobe shacks high in the Andes mountains, twelve hours' frightening and dangerous drive from Lima.

Writing a friend, Murray expressed a new concern: "Another problem, one which has concerned me all along . . . is the problem of securing adequate Christian leadership. Closely tied in . . . appears to be the difficult task of continually broadening our outreach, taking in more students, reaching more new ones rather than contenting ourselves with one group."

His philosophy was changing! "I do not mean," he continued, "that I think we should strive for the hordes or ignore the ones we have; rather I think we should strive to make our program so intensive that it will catch and hold the ones we have, and for that, bring more in. Seeing Latin America has made me more definitely sure of exactly what the church ought to try to accomplish and of the absolute necessity of doing it."

The die was cast. Dr. Hall said later, "On his trip Murray found that some of the things which were essential to him were not really essential. He changed his position and matured."

Enthusiastic impressions were given to the officials of the Methodist Board of Missions, and some eyebrows must have been raised over the detailed and analytical report Murray delivered. Among those impressed with his reports from the mission field and genuinely interested in recruiting him was Dr. Alfred Wasson, executive secretary for Latin America of the Methodist Board of Missions. Knowing Murray from previous Texas contacts, Dr. Wasson directed their conversation more pointedly toward implications for Murray's future.

His head in a whirl and the recent experiences not completely organized in his thinking, Murray fired off a letter to his beloved friend Dr. Hall, in Austin. Recognizing Murray's capacity for service in the church on a very wide scale, Dr. Hall emphasized what he saw in the young man in one paragraph of the letter he returned immediately:

> The work here, as you know, is rather confining for a man who has the ability to do the things you have been doing. There are many things which seem trivial. Someone must see that these are done. ... With a man of your ability ... you an scarcely push aside the claims that are laid upon you by the whole church. It may be that you have advanced to the point at which it would be impossible for you to return to your work as director or associate director. ... Perhaps you have already been ruined for such a position, not in the sense of being unable to do the work, but in the sense of reaching a point where outside demands are too great and too numerous for you to stick to the routines of a local worker. Do not think I am inconsiderate of you in any manner. I am merely trying in a very frank manner to present the many angles and help you see the whole picture.

The letter helped. From it came one of Murray's pet expressions, "You have to see the big picture."

Decisions still lay ahead in hours of prayerful consideration. Totally immersing himself in the spring activities of the student center in Austin, Murray still found many hours to be alone and consider his problem as he sought reasonable solutions.

Uncle Sam helped when Murray was requested to return the Selective Service questionnaire on which his classification would be based. His satisfactory work in the Wesley Foundation had resulted in a vote by the Board of Directors to support him and in a petition to the draft board to allow him to continue his work with students.

Pressure was mounting in the alert, active, and searching mind. On the occasion of his mother's birthday he wrote a touching letter in which he reassured his mother that he had little to give her exept an expression of gratitude for what his parents had given him. He affirmed his belief in the ultimate triumph of right, goodness, and square play and honesty and in the fundamental dignity of all humans. He added, "I want you to know that your son believes in God. He may not believe in the same kind of God he grew up believing in, but he does believe in God, very really and vitally and that is what matters."

42

Murray's thinking was taking shape. Again Uncle Sam forced decision. An appearance before the draft board resulted in the IV-E classification as a conscientious objector. He was haunted by the fear of doing nothing worthwhile in a CO camp.

The possibility of entering theology school and preparing for more creative use of his talents in the period of reconstruction seemed more logical. Then another alternative materialized. A concrete idea took shape in the form of missionary work in South America!

The possibility of entering theology school had smacked of easy solution. He had been urged by the draft board to register as a minister of The Methodist Church and was assured that he was more a minister than many whom they had so classified. But his reply had been, "I am not good enough to be a minister."

Mission work in South America was practical, and it would answer the need he felt to do something constructive in lieu of being drafted or spending wasted time in a CO camp.

By mid-April a decision seemed to be near. Writing his parents he said, "I am still not finally settled on where I go from here, but I am pretty well decided that it will either be Vanderbilt [theology school] or Peru. Anyhow, I am happier now than I have been in a long time."

NOVA

A further cause for Murray's happiness was not immediately obvious to those around him. Always meticulously prompt, it was noticed that Murray's pattern changed with spring. Whereas previously he had always been counted on to be at his desk well ahead of everyone else, now he began to appear later and later. It was only a matter of time until his reason was discovered; each morning he was walking Nova Bryant to the school where she was teaching.

Only a few days after indicating his decision had narrowed to theology school or Peru, a simple line in a letter read, "We have our minds definitely made up that we want to do missionary work."

The "we" signaled the beginning of a team approach to both mission-field work and a life's devotion. It began in a student conference in Kansas. Nova described it in brief words: "A tall, slender, handsome young man walked in with a young lady on his arm. He walked in, and my freedom was gone forever. I didn't know it then, but the next two years would be the most miserable in my life and the twenty after that would be the most filled years. I was in love and hoped that I'd meet that young man."

They didn't meet immediately, but after they returned to Austin, Nova received a letter inviting her to drop in to the Wesley Foundation and perhaps find a place to use her talents in the drama program. She did stop and was ushered into the office where Murray sat with his back to her. When he stood up and turned around, Nova smiled weakly and groped for a chair. She remembers nothing of what she promised, but the courtship began.

There had been many young ladies, but none had ever received the kind of attention that Murray gave Nova. Love at first sight was not Murray's way of doing things. After many dates, sharing in discussion groups, and long walks after various services and programs, over a period of two years Murray awakened to the realization that what lay behind the blue and piercing eyes was a deep love which enabled Nova to understand and share the burden of struggle in which he was caught.

During one extremely painful period for Nova, Murray was rumored to have fallen for a lovely Bolivian girl. He did admit to a quick flirtation. Nova forgave the "fling" and continued to solicitously help Murray analyze alternatives confronting him.

Despairing of anything permanent coming of her feelings for Murray, Nova allowed her friendship with a Yankee boy to progress to the point of an engagement. Years later, in his typically humorous way, Murray accused Nova of using a Yankee to entice a "perfectly good Texan." The engagement was finally broken, and Murray and Nova grew closer and closer.

In the touchy period of decision making, Nova held her patience in check until Murray came to the realization of her affection for him. No decision was easy for him during that period of his life, and deciding to ask Nova to marry him was complicated by his many problems with the draft, an uncertainty about what he would do, and what Nova would be called on to do if she did marry him.

In long springtime walks, Murray talked, and Nova listened. Her understanding and patient listening helped her know Murray's deep integrity. Their love grew in the soil of perfect frankness and complete understanding.

Finally, within a two-week period the decisions had been made. Nova insists that the proposal was all one sentence: "Will you marry me and go to South America as a missionary?" The proposal was one of love, but it was more. It was a call to share in a dedication that was growing. The serious, idealistic young man proposed marriage and the possibilities of hardship and sacrifice to the beautiful young lady who had known and enjoyed the substantial and comfortable things in life.

Confusion again reigned. Orders were received for Murray to report to the CO camp at Magnolia, Arkansas. At the same time he was processing new applications for the Methodist Board of Missions, including that of Nova, his future wife.

Nova knew the implications of the CO camp. In a gentle way Murray had suggested that if she wished, she could call the whole thing off. She looked at him and said, "Well, four years is little enough we can do for Christ. How soon can we be married?"

It was not as simple as it sounded. Nova's father, an employee of the government, held views exactly opposite to those of Murray. Knowing of Mr. Bryant's objections, Murray arranged, at some exertion of time and effort, to see him. Across cups of coffee Murray expressed his love for Nova and the personal convictions which compelled him.

At the wedding Mr. Bryant confided to Dr. Heinsohn, "When Murray found out that I was unhappy, he called for a conference and sat across from me. I could not agree with him, but had to respect him. It takes more courage to do what Murray is doing than to wear a uniform and parade when bands are playing and flags are waving. I do respect him."

The wedding took place at University Methodist Church in Austin on May 30, 1942, with Drs. Hall and Heinsohn officiating.

Typical of things to come, the honeymoon was spent at a summer conference where Murray was the speaker. Kerrville was a familiar place to Murray, but the cabin in which they spent their first few days together was different from any place he had ever known. Nova's love brought out in him an obvious radiance. Upon arrival at the camp, they discovered a note on the door, "Welcome home—Murray and Nova."

From Mt. Wesley the couple moved on to Dallas where they took summer courses at the Southern Methodist School of Theology in preparation for their chosen missionary work.

Uncertainty had plagued the couple until the moment of the wedding. In a series of fast-moving events Murray had submitted to a physical examination as directed by the draft board. Ironically he was declared as physically unfit for the service by examining doctors. While all this was transpiring, he attempted one final effort to serve honorably and applied for noncombatant status. That application was refused. Faith and intuition proved correct; they were finally approved by the Board of Missions of The Methodist Church for work in South America.

Guided by the counsel of Dr. Wasson, who was on the S.M.U. campus that summer, Nova and Murray anticipated further preparation. Any South American appointment meant some time studying either at Yale University or at the Kennedy School of Missions in Hartford, Connecticut. While Murray and Nova spent the last part of the summer appearing in summer camps, the decisions were forwarded from New York. From Dr. Wasson came the word: they were to be assigned to Cochabamba, Bolivia.

A quick trip to New York on September 14, 1942, resulted in final aceptance by the Board of Missions. They were referred to the Hartford Seminary Foundation, where Murray discovered old friends from previous student conferences. With the acceptance of the Dicksons also came a grant relieving some of the financial strain. Murray was given a part-time job at Hillyer Junior College. His weekends were filled with speaking engagements throughout the area within several hundred miles of Hartford.

The couple were eager and enthusiastic as they made the final preparations for their trip south. The course of studies prepared them to understand the socio-economic conditions of Latin America. In addition, the philosophy of missions was examined in detail. Mastering Spanish was another story. Murray took to it easily; Nova struggled until she suddenly realized that it was far easier than she had convinced herself it was.

Plans for their travel were initiated. Wartime restrictions made it necessary to plan well in advance and then still not be certain of last-minute details. They were nearing the end of their schooling when word reached them that another step into the ministry had been taken for Murray. Dr. Heinsohn wrote to advise Murray that on the strength of his simple letter of inquiry about the steps toward qualifying for ordination and license to preach, his circumstance had been taken up by the proper committee, and he had been admitted on trial into the Southwest Texas Conference of The Methodist Church in absentia.

Not all in Austin had shared Murray's convictions. As a target for many cruel taunts because of his pacifist persuasions, Murray had spared no effort to convince his adversaries of his integrity. When the news was made known that Murray was to go to South America as a missionary, a self-styled patriot authored the rumor that Murray was "being run out of the country." Rising to Murray's defense, several friends attempted to set the superpatriot straight. In the fickle wartime setting they could do little to change the falsely circulated rumors. Many years later the author of the rumor happened into a place where Murray was speaking. Following the speech he approached Murray and apologized for his earlier mistaken accusations.

Murray's comments to his father reveal the underlying uncertainty he felt about his ordination: "It is hard to explain exactly my feelings in this matter. I have always been interested in church work . . . but somehow I never before felt quite worthy to be called a minister. Nor do I feel worthy now . . . yet the fact that I now have ministerial status means a great deal to me."

Within the letter he revealed that as long as he was not finally classified by the draft board, he could not seek ministerial status for fear it would have appeared to be an escape.

On their way to commissioning in Cleveland, Ohio, as missionaries, Murray and Nova carried the first letters from missionary personnel on the field in Bolivia telling them a little of what they could expect when they arrived in Cochabamba.

Mildred and LeGrande Smith had been in Cochabamba several years and were well qualified to suggest the items Murray and Nova ought to include in their careful packing. Nova was warned that if she intended to have a family while in Bolivia, she should go prepared with a supply of "little things." In letters to Texas she assured her family they could help her in that category, and whatever they offered could be packed and taken with great glee. She confidently announced that she expected to return from her first term with two grandchildren for the family to spoil.

Another letter, coveted for many years because of the wealth of precise information, came from Laveta Hobson. Her suggestions were parallel those of the Smiths, and the letters complemented each other. Nova began packing according to the very strict regulations supplied to aid her.

The apprentice missionaries had had enough of northern winters as they left Hartford for a brief trip to Texas. One final obstacle confronted them: their passports had not been cleared. Upon inquiry they were advised that there were no more passports, and they would be advised when they could apply again.

Rising to a high pitch of action, Murray shot off a telegram to Washington expressing his ire and indicating that he had seen news that three hundred Maryknoll priests were leaving for South America. If they could have passports, why could not he? He asked why his rights as a citizen were being treated lightly. He also enlisted the aid of several influential Austin friends from the political scene. Within three days the passports were in his hands. All that remained was notification of the sailing date.

THE
JOURNEY
SOUTH

New Orleans was a beehive of activity. Gray ships were loading cargoes furiously as if there was a chance their ghostlike appearance might change, and someone would discover that they were a part of the war. Once aboard ship Murray and Nova submitted to the tension which permeated everything.

While sailing to Cuba, an airplane flew constantly above the convoy of ships. As they entered Guantanamo Bay, they observed a familiar bustle and feverish pitch of work. After leaving Cuba they sailed for Panama. A few hours away from land Nova was completely unnerved when, during an abandon-ship drill, a merchant marine asked her, "How's your heart?" Then to one of his mates he said, "You take the lady to lifeboat ten. I'll wake the gentleman [Murray] and take him to nine."

Reports of submarines kept everybody on tense alert. To ease the situation Nova and another woman dressed in their prettiest gowns for dinner that first evening out of Guantanamo. Soon after dark a plane flew low over the convoy and dropped depth charges a few miles away. Simultaneously two ships on the horizon exploded and lighted the entire area.

Once through the Panama Canal, some of the tension eased as the threat of submarines greatly lessened. Then Murray and Nova discovered another kind of problem. Several couples from fundamentalist theological persuasions offered very frank disapproval of their conduct during the submarine scare, including the style of dress the women had worn. So marked, Murray and Nova were snubbed by the straitlaced missionaries for the remainder of the trip.

The friendly and easygoing Murray sought to offend no one and enjoyed some of the common pleasures which were held to be sinful by the more fundamentalist brothers. To occupy time, Murray organized discussion groups. Once his rather liberal views were voiced, the lines were drawn even tighter.

Aiding in conducting worship aboard ship and counseling lonely merchant marines who had been at sea for long periods also took considerable time.

It was years before Murray could laugh at one incident within a worship service just before they entered the Panama Canal. With tension at its worst, one of the fundamentalist missionaries with a beautiful voice sang the solo, "Rocked in the Cradle of the Deep." All his hatred of war, the pressures of anxiety, and his fears for Nova's safety were almost more than Murray could stand. His violent reaction was kept to himself, except for Nova's perceptive observation.

Doubtless some of the early enthusiasm for the voyage was dulled by wartime shortages, lack of water, and the generally severe conditions. Still the novice missionaries looked forward to anchoring off the port of Arica, Chile, and watching as small boats and barges ventured out into deep water where they received cargoes to be taken to the shallow-water docks. Nova and Murray had visions of all their belongings being dumped into the deep Pacific, as sometimes happened.

Landing on solid ground after three weeks aboard ship, the two found that their train for La Paz would leave just after sundown. Taking in the last of the sunset on the Pacific, they boarded the train, which throughout the night wound up and through the Andes. The morning found Murray looking out the window at majestic, rose-tinted, snow-covered mountain peaks all around him.

For hours the scenery entranced the two flatland Texans as they observed the grotesquely beautiful Andes. Reaching the altiplano, they got their first glimpses of llamas, alpacas, and occasionally the graceful but skittish vicuña. The brightly colored dress of the natives made them conspicuous against the drab, brownish altiplano.

It was late afternoon when at the edge of the altiplano Murray and Nova saw what captivates every first-time viewer. La Paz gleamed in the last rays of the afternoon sun. Overlooking the scene from its lofty perch many miles away but seeming to be just beyond the reach of one's arm was Illimani, the magnificent mountain.

Dr. and Mrs. Beck waited for them an hour later at the 12,000-foot level. They were secure in the custody of the couple who would attend them medically and act almost as parents for many years.

Renewing their previous friendship with Murray, the Becks also demonstrated concern for Nova. At the clinic they provided the first warm bath she had seen for three weeks. That bath stands out as one of the grandest moments of her life. Inconveniences and handicaps were to become commonplace to the enthusiastic couple.

Poor news met them in La Paz. Heavy rains had washed out the railroad between La Paz and Cochabamba. Delayed in La Paz for several days, with service restored on Saturday instead of Monday, Dr. and Mrs.

Beck put Murray and Nova on the train for the trip to Cochabamba. Even more fascinated than on the trip from Arica to La Paz because this was their new country, the couple took careful interest in the people along the way, noting changes in costumes, especially the headdress of the Indians.

Crossing the last section of the altiplano, Murray took notes and wrote careful descriptions of the antics of the wind where it had full, unimpeded sweep of the vast stretches of flat land at 13,000 feet. Often as many as twenty whirlwinds were reported by Murray, who wrote the account to send to friends in Texas. The account reported vivid details from each stop and the appearance of the people as viewed from the train.

As the train entered the Cochabamba Valley in the late evening, it made a stop. At that point LeGrande Smith, Sr., boarded the train and struggling from coach to coach over piles of cargo and disarrayed Indians, finally found Murray and Nova. The occasion was filled with delight and emotion. Murray and Nova were the first missionaries to enter Bolivia from the former southern branch of The Methodist Church. The nervous, tired, and anxious missionaries neared their destination.

Twenty miles farther on, the train slowed to a stop in the Cochabamba station. As they left the train, a group of seventy-five students, on hand for the arrival of the new missionaries, broke into a heavily accented rendition of "Yankee Doodle Dandy." After a round of traditional "abrazos" (a chest-to-chest embrace and handshake), they led Murray and Nova down the main street with shouts of "Rah—rah for de Deek-sons."

At the school more students joined in the welcome, and more shouts rang through the peaceful city. None of the letters from the States had preceded them; neither had airmail letters sent from Cuba. The only warning of the exact arrival of the Dicksons had been the short message which Dr. Beck had sent from La Paz that morning on the national telegraph system, "just in case." Murray noted that bit of thoughtfulness and made it a strict personal policy to be sure that every last "just in case" detail was provided for those whose safety was his responsibility.

A day had not been time enough to put things in order, so the first item of business facing Murray and Nova was making their living quarters in the school livable.

INTO
the VALLEY
of COCHABAMBA

On the long, dirty, and inconvenient trip the crude passenger cars were crowded with Indians who never bathed and a variety of other pungent and penetrating odors. Expectation, eagerness, and the enthusiastic welcome left Murray and Nova emotionally and physically exhausted. The 9,000-foot altitude was a welcome relief, as it would be to Murray whenever he traveled from the extremes of nearly sea level to sometimes 17,000 feet without benefit of oxygen.

Anticipating opportunity to refresh themselves, they arrived at the school which would be their home for several years. Among the first to greet them were two single women serving faithfully as teaching missionaries. The humor of their welcome did not occur to the others as it struck the dirty, travel-weary couple: "We don't have any water, since we had to give the dog a bath this evening."

A wonderful beginning! Then things began to get

even more interesting. A careful explanation indicated that their permanent rooms would not be ready for a few days. The rooms housed a temporary infirmary accommodating several serious cases of ringworm among the "internas" or girl boarding students. With that bit of news, the couple shared another deep breath and look of unbelief.

Finally deposited in a hastily furnished dwelling, as soon as the door was closed and they were given privacy, Murray gathered Nova into his arms and kissed her while they laughed at the confused situations which had befallen them. They were both still weak from laughing when Murray sat down on the bed to take off his shoes. The bed promptly collapsed, unceremoniously spilling suitcases, clothing, and Murray on the floor. The ensuing laughter was convulsive. Their arrival was complete.

Early Sunday morning they retrieved their personal effects from under a mountain of crates, various trunks, and other shipping cartons which had been ingloriously dumped from the baggage cars late the night before. No motorized vehicles were to be found, so their baggage was loaded on a small-wheeled, man-drawn cart. The cost was ridiculously small. The scene was so foreign to the novice missionaries that Murray was prompted to remark that they had become the Bolivian parallel to the scene from the American novel *Grapes of Wrath*.

The new arrivals fell into established routines with amazing rapidity. It was all new, yet taken so much in stride by the older, more experienced people that Murray and Nova marveled. Monday was a regular school day. Its greatest impression was stamped in Murray's mind when he was returning from the purchase of a newspaper on the street. He was surprised to find a boy about twelve years of age who had dropped his bundle of cargo and was using bare feet to climb the adobe walls so he could peer through the barred windows at classes in session.

This scene of a youngster shut out from education and yet eager to see what went on in a classroom left a profound impression on Murray. He often re-created this scene in words as an introductory illustration to the needs of Bolivia.

The second day of their work the local officials had declared as a holiday to welcome Vice-President Henry Wallace from the United States. On Monday an official had visited the school and requested that they make 2,000 American flags for the welcome. When it was explained that such a project would call for cutting of 96,000 stars and 14,000 red and 12,000 white stripes, the official compromised on 150 flags. These were made ready when school was dismissed early the morning of the Vice-President's visit. Meanwhile Nova was busy thoroughly disinfecting the vacated infirmary which would be their home.

Seeing the American Institute (the name given to Methodist Mission Schools in Bolivia) Vice-President Wallace ordered his car stopped, and he entered the school. Bolivian people were startled. Speaking in a deliberate Spanish, the Vice-President made a great impression on his own countrymen as well as on the Bolivians who watched his obvious efforts at goodwill.

The demands of true, genteel Spanish hospitality were soon evident to the new missionaries when at the end of their first eight days they could count back to welcoming activities of three teas, a luncheon, three public meetings, and innumerable individual visits by which they were honored and welcomed.

Teaching began almost immediately. Both Murray and Nova were soon immersed in their classroom and in additional activities. Countless projects occurred to them. The physical facilities were in poor repair. The classrooms were always in need of some new and attractive display to supplement a current teaching unit. Students came forward guardedly to make friends with the young teacher with warm eyes so like Bolivian eyes. His Spanish was surprisingly good, and he felt up to using it in his first speech before the school at an assembly.

Living accommodations kept both husband and wife busy. Murray described their living quarters in a letter to home: "Our apartment opens onto the reception patio of the school on one side and into the garden on the other, so that we have delightful privacy. In order not to exaggerate, I have just measured again to find that our thinnest outside wall is five feet thick, and the walls between the rooms are no thinner—in fact there is practically a hallway connecting each room with the next. The ceilings are eleven feet and more above the floor."

The letter continued with a vivid description of the collection of makeshift trunks, boxes, and old chairs which made up their home. Murray credited Nova with transforming the rooms into very livable quarters with the use of curtains and other bright materials. It was their first real home since marrying. It would be the scene of many happy moments as well as shelter in face of considerable anxiety.

During the initial period of responsibility, the Dicksons ate with the "internas." Also sharing the responsibility for student conduct at meals were the two single ladies. Periodically relations between the two women grew strained, and a cold, stony silence ensued at the table where they ate with Murray and Nova. It became too funny to endure long when Nova or Murray would be asked by one to pass along a message to the other so they could avoid direct communication, yet still let their wishes be known.

A sense of humor became one of the most important tools in approaching both work and personal relationships. Bolivian ways often defied logic, but Murray's most sterling quality—his patience—saved many a difficult situation from becoming dangerous or unhappy. Even when on furlough, Murray's keen sense of humor enabled him to recall specific incidents and humorously contrast the Bolivian scene to that known by his North American audiences.

The farmboy turned missionary found himself painfully involved in a society he did not understand. As he worked to understand the complexities of Bolivia, he stored up a vast reservoir of information. Wherever he went, his eye was continually caught by evidence of poverty and the evils of a society built for the comfort and convenience of the wealthy.

Murray was moved when he found common men living in squalor or confined by obstacles which prevented them from earning a livelihood and self-respect. His willingness to share and identify with those unfortunates is shown in the countless nights spent in undesirable sleeping accommodations provided by those who offered their best.

The crusade mounted steadily in Murray from the moment he began to analyze conditions in the Cochabamba Valley. It grew as he prepared for the day when he could bring improvements to the common man. Years of close relationships and intimate knowledge of the circumstances of ordinary men gave Murray a sensitive frame of reference when speaking where influential Bolivian leadership listened.

Only a few days after arriving in Cochabamba, Murray began to share with many men the desire to view the valley from Tunari, the high mountain which overlooked Cochabamba. He inquired of many if they had climbed the imposing peak. Finding that few had, but many dreamed of doing so, the pioneer in Murray aimed toward the day when he would stand on the peak and view the peaceful valley he had chosen as home. When he did make the ascent, it was with several Bolivians in the party to share the exhilarating experience.

Murray Dickson loved people. In the market he took time and made an effort to be polite to vendors. In hotels he thanked doormen. Those considered by others as servants were objects of his attention and affection. Few persons met Murray without revealing some morsel of information about family or pressing personal problems. From such knowledge grew a personal interest, and the next encounter resulted in a question about the family or pressing problem.

Murray's genuine interest and natural curiosity never abated. Newspaper vendors, shoeshine boys, waiters in coffee shops, and others from humble servant positions provided an insight into the average Bolivian's needs, hungers, and thirsts.

Harsh censors made communication with the United States precarious as they stripped letters of any information which might have aided enemy—or family, as it often seemed. Letters were events. Each letter listed items of special importance from previous notes to assure some degree of continuity.

Mailing a letter was a task of skill. Very primitive methods used in the Cochabamba post office called for purchase of stamps at one window, then taking the stamped envelope to another window where the canceling was done. A final trip placed the letter in a relatively secure position for dispatch. Often the employees steamed stamps from uncancelled letters and resold the stamps on the street.

Bureaucracy prevailed everywhere. All travel called for permits. In his earliest experiences Murray learned to exercise patience. Each successive negotiation in the various offices developed a confidence on the part of officials in this outgoing young missionary.

Dishonesty, petty theft, cheating, and various forms of unethical conduct were evident in the street and shop as well as in the classroom. A promise from Murray Dickson was soon discovered to be completely reliable. He often went out of his way to fulfill a promise made to an obscure clerk.

Away from the city, Murray became more sympathetic with the conditions of the common man. The farmer in his temperament enabled him to admire good farming and fine livestock and to converse with common men in tropical as well as high mountain areas of Bolivia. Men sensed his down-to-earth approach to life through his genuine interest in things of the soil.

Not all men Murray met were of low estate. Very early in his work in Cochabamba he became interested in Rotary International. Working in the club, he soon found himself president of the group and gained the friendship of many influential citizens and leaders of Cochabamba.

In government offices where he presented his cause before stern and authoritarian officials, they were won by Murray's warm, logical approach. Encountering outright hostility was common, but he seldom left an office without having made both his point and a new friend. Murray Dickson had the happy faculty of approaching a man to ask a favor and leaving with that person begging Murray to allow him the privilege.

Where Murray met unbending hostility because he represented The Methodist Church, he still managed to garner a degree of respect which demanded thoughtful consideration.

Among Murray's responsibilities was the constant search for new property on which the school could rebuild. The old buildings on Plaza Colon were in a seriously deteriorated condition. The hunt progressed for a year without success. Every possible lead was investigated and purchase proposed. On several occasions when it looked like negotiations were about to be concluded, complications caused the deals to fall through. On at least six occasions priests of the Catholic Church threatened to excommunicate members if they sold land to Methodists.

During these periods of searching, Murray came to know the city thoroughly. He could quickly use the shortest route through the narrow and winding streets. This knowledge was to save his life or at least prevent serious injury during several difficult revolutionary periods of the late 1940's and early 1950's. Reporting his explorations, Murray told of examining more than thirty lots, discussing price with twenty owners and entering into negotiations with six.

Exposed to the labyrinthine ways of Bolivian real estate law, Murray exercised more patience than ever. One property seemed most desirable. The seller was persuaded by a devout Catholic sister that he should not sell. Later a son with power of attorney let it be known that the lot was for sale. As soon as he could, Murray worked with LeGrande Smith to arrange "aras." This meant that if the school did not conclude the sale, they lost the aras. If the owner refused to conclude, he had to pay back the aras along with an equal amount of indemnity.

To celebrate the purchase of the land, a big picnic was held on the new property. With funds advanced for purchase, the problems began of finding both financing for the building and building materials. Wartime shortages caused delays or made substitutions of materials a necessity. All avenues of help were investigated. Officials of the Bolivian government and representatives of the U. S. Embassy offered sympathy but no concrete help or solution during the long, strenuous period.

When Murray became discouraged over the slow progress or was even remotely tempted to give up, he was stopped by the haunting picture of the common

man whose dim hopes depended upon him, and with renewed energy he worked harder than ever.

A reputation for hard work, kindly patience, and
common sense soon preceded Murray. In unswerving
honesty he met every problem and situation with the
same interested warmth. Throughout the city people
began to respect the hard-working young man.

Students weren't beyond testing him to find out how
far they could press a man of such integrity and
patience. Soon after beginning a course on the teachings of Jesus, Murray delighted to notice a student
with hand raised who inquired if he might ask a
question. Murray could not understand the hesitation.
He encouraged the boy to ask any question at all. "Is
it a sin to read the New Testament? One of the professors at LaSalle [a neighboring Catholic school] took
a New Testament from a boy and tore it up and threw
it on the floor saying it was the work of the devil!"

Murray was shocked. He stated that it was not a sin.
In the United States, Roman Catholics were encouraged
to read a new version just printed. The students insisted that they had heard priests condemn reading of
the Bible.

Writing Dr. Wasson, Murray told of this first real
shock to his spirit of "sweetness and light" concerning
relations between Catholic and Protestant branches of

the church. "Then I very tactlessly suggested that the priests might have had a reason for their statements. In Brazil, for example, the people were forbidden to read the New Testament because the religion of the times could not stand the comparison. The class ended with the students insisting that the Pope himself had forbidden the reading of the New Testament."

The letter continues as it best relates the story: "That afternoon I set out for Calacala, a suburb in which some of the Maryknoll missionaries from the United States are at work. I found one of the fathers. He assured me . . . . The Roman Catholic Church did not like for its people to read non-Catholic versions . . . but it was not a sin to read a Catholic version. Indeed the Pope urged people to read the Bible. Then he told me of a similar interesting experience of his own."

Murray related the story that the priest was discovered by one of his students reading the Bible. He had told the priest he was mistaken to read such an evil book. The priest then took out the missal and showed him that almost every phrase of the mass came from either New or Old Testament.

The friendly visit ended when Murray offered to buy Catholic versions of the New Testament if the priest would secure them for him. As Murray left, the priest admitted that Bolivian priests had forbidden reading of the Bible in Protestant versions but had neglected to make Catholic versions available.

Most disturbing of all was the final admission which Murray quoted as the young priest's confession: "I am ashamed to say it, but you are doing more for the religious development of these Catholic boys and girls than most of their own priests. It is for that reason that there are twenty of us here from one mission school in Bolivia as missionaries, not to the jungles, but to the cities, for the Papal Nuncio has asked for missionaries to the centers of culture as well as to the periphery."

The closing lines of the letter detailing this encounter gave indication of the problems which would confront Murray in his attempts to educate and help the Bolivian people: "Daily we are more convinced of the desperate need of mission work in this country. Even such elemental virtues as honesty and truth-telling are lacking, apparently not taught at all by the established church here. The most dishonest girls we have here in the internada [boarding school] are some who have spent most of their lives in a Catholic convent school and home."

Dishonesties, inconsistencies, and the carefully laid systems of ethics peculiar to Bolivia came quickly to the attention of the bright, enthusiastic, and optimistic missionaries. Murray remained cautiously open and sympathetic to the problems of Roman Catholic priests from the United States when they attempted to be ethical. In private conversation this concern for their situation was communicated in a quiet friendship on the part of a number of North American priests. Not until after Pope John XXIII's initiative resulted in opened channels of communication could the priests freely admit their friendship and admiration for Murray and the work of The Methodist Church in Bolivia.

Before this happened, the work of The Methodist Church in education would expand in great strides. Sensing such growth, the bishop presiding over Cochabamba issued a letter stating that all families with children enrolled in Methodist schools would be excommunicated from the church. Fearful that this would hurt the school, Murray was relieved by the approach of a man who had two children in the Methodist school and two others in a Catholic school. Questioned about his fear over the threat, the man replied to Murray, "By experience we know now that they get more than a good education in your school. They also learn how to live. Don't worry about the bishop. I can get around that."

Prejudicies and problems born of ignorance on the part of suspicious Bolivian national priests created great obstacles for the rapidly growing Protestant churches. Most of Murray's twenty years of work were spent in a state of undeclared war between the two groups. Often North American priests appeared to side with the Protestant groups. Every possible method of provoking discouragement was attempted by the more militant Roman Catholics. Murray found it in government negotiations, in customs officials who stymied the entry of badly needed equipment, and frequently in the lower ranks of clerks who used the maze of bureaucracy to slow procedures. As time passed, more graduates and friends of The Methodist Church secured positions where they could be counted on to provide a liaison for the church and to expedite paper work, thus speeding the liberation processes.

At the time of Pope John XXIII's declarations of ecumenism, Murray observed with unusual pessimism, "It is too good to be true. If he [Pope John] can even persuade them to talk to us he will have accomplished one of the great miracles of the Christian church, but even then, it will take a century to get this attitude of acceptance to Bolivia's common man." His experience had taught the bitter lessons of rivalry and deeply ingrained traditions to which Catholicism appealed in a nation where very few had the opportunity of education, but where everyone was subjected to the pressures of superstition and a mixture of pagan and Christian belief.

Murray experienced several demonstrations in both La Paz and Cochabamba in which Roman Catholic priests, along with their students, led the march and threw stones at Methodist schools. He experienced firsthand the outward expressions of fear at the threat which the Catholic Church saw in Protestantism.

Everywhere Murray turned during the first years, he found the mingled pagan and superstitious Catholic influence upon the common man. He first encountered the dogma of San Juan when he decided to burn some trash on the new property. Setting fire to it, he was soon gasping for breath when one of the helpers sagely advised, "You should invoke San Juan's aid."

A little puzzled, Murray inquired further. The explanation was that San Juan was the patron saint of fire. In setting out to find the origin of this concept, he also learned that the ancient Incas designated a time corresponding to June 21 as the longest night of the year and used that date to begin a fiesta to honor the sun. They kindled new fires on every hearth, set fire to whatever would burn on the hillsides, and sought to make the longest night of the year pass quickly. Spanish priests, unable to stamp out the tradition, altered it to serve their purpose.

Together the priests began declaring it a fiesta in honor of St. John. It was done so consistently over a period of time, with an appeal to the priest's right to interpretation, that eventually the pagan origins were forgotten. The tradition persists today. Even in La Paz, the traveler does well to avoid that 13,000-foot elevation during the Dia San Juan celebration because of the bonfires which use up precious oxygen and fill the valley with dense smoke.

Probably most disturbing to Murray of all the inherent problems of the Catholic Church was the lack of a social conscience on the part of the church and as a result the complete lack of such concern on the part of the people. It took very little time to recognize the alliance between the Catholic Church and the government; there was also a very evident attachment between the wealthy and the church. An "establishment" had been created over the years by which the church was party to the evils of poverty and a definite caste system within the population.

In a long-range look at the problems between Roman Catholicism and Protestantism in Bolivia, Murray said, "If we [Protestants] do nothing else in South America, we can take pride in the fact that we have pricked the conscience of the masses of people who call themselves Christian and Catholic but have ignored social problems. I see a definite rise in social concern among the youth and the students which will carry over into coming generations. Almost without exception this trend and movement has been the result of the Protestant Church working in Latin America."

Change was the order of the day for twenty years. By the time of his death, even though they could not attend his funeral openly, Catholic priests who had worked where they could observe the leadership of Murray Dickson would express to his close friends their frank grief at the loss of one who, though critical of their church, was both fair and understanding and known to go beyond expected limits to extend cooperation in fraternal and professional courtesies.

There were many problems other than church relationships to be dealt with, however. Once in the classroom Murray and Nova were subject to severe shock. Teaching methods were deplorable. Only when permitted opportunity to investigate public schools and other parochial schools were they convinced that the best possible job was being done in their own mission school.

They discovered that almost all teaching was done by rote. Since books were very expensive and only occasionally available, the teacher spent most of the time dictating materials for "cuadernos" or notebooks from which the student could later study. Teaching aids were almost nonexistent. Maps, if available, were ancient and tattered. Only by personal ingenuity did most professors make their subjects live. A good teacher found employment in as many as three schools, drawing full salary from each. Even then, his income was miserably low. Pioneering work of The Methodist Church in education included the raising of teachers' salaries. This also provided for securing the best available teachers.

Frequent interruption of the school schedule was dictated by the Ministry of Education, which had complete control of the schools, public and private. They set the schedule, determined the curriculum, and frequently, to make a show of their authority, called all schools together for a mass convocation. Some were rather perfunctory, being called suddenly, as Murray noted in a letter from mid-1943. He said that his school was notified to report to the central plaza, along with all other schools. The event turned out to be an address by the head of the local university on the subject, "The Origin and Evolution of Man." The subject evoked an immediate outcry of protest, and slowly the listening crowd dwindled until very few students remained in the plaza which had at one time been a sea of black heads. Those who retreated went home, and another day of school was wasted.

Murray found it difficult to believe that he would permit a travesty on education in his own classroom such as that which he encountered in final examinations. But law was law, and he could do little except seethe quietly. The examination procedure was designed to keep everyone honest, but frequently it managed just the opposite. Murray's description and comments show his disgust with the situation which he labored faithfully over the years to adjust and simplify:

The final examinations here are a tragedy. The government office sends two "delegates" from other schools, often persons who try to injure the records of the schools they examine so that their own will do well by comparison. These two delegates and the professors constitute a tribunal; the classes are called in and one by one . . . in alphabetical order as prescribed by law . . . following a previously approved list . . . each student is questioned. Each of the delegates and the professors makes a note of the examination responses. . . . At the end of the last examination the delegates and professors assemble in the school office together with the secretary and director of the school. Drinks are served (beer and wine in most, soda pop in ours). The secretary seats herself before a huge book called

"Libro de Examines" (Examination Book). The delegates seat themselves on either side of the secretary; the secretary then calls the name of the student, the first delegate calls his examination grade, the second calls his. The secretary enters them in the respective columns. Then she averages the two examination grades . . . with the term average given by the teacher and puts the final grade in the last column.

Then each delegate . . . the professor . . . and finally the director of the school signs each page. The book, with all grades from all classes and subjects in the school, is then taken to the headquarters of the scholastic district. I have never seen a more elaborate or useless ceremony . . . none more unfair . . . some of my students who should have busted out got by with good grades and others who knew the material well were frightened and unable to tell what they knew.

With final examinations like this behind them, the newcomers were considered veterans, and they entered into another segment of life which would be new to them.

The newly established veterans maintained a rigid and costly discipline of honor and integrity. War conditions throughout the world, scarcity of important materials, and a variety of other complications made the task of maintaining a school in the mission field nearly a superhuman effort. As bookkeeper, LeGrande Smith, Sr., was a master comptroller. For months preceding the arrival of the Dicksons, he and the other missionary personnel had sold their salary checks to the school at below par exchange rate to help add to the funds with which to administer the school. Murray and Nova immediately joined the system, thus sacrificing their purchasing power, but assuring financial resources for the school. It was discovered that on at least one occasion the sacrifice had been so complete that Mr. Smith had had to borrow money to buy shoes for his children.

Money was not the only constant problem. Health had to be carefully watched and was preserved only by the strictest precautions. When it first became evident that Nova was pregnant, it became more necessary to watch their diet. Even then an occasional case of "Cochabamba belly," a nickname for a severe intestinal infection, would nearly cripple one. Some illnesses were short, others more prolonged. Occasionally the infection was so severe as to cause actual paralysis of the lower abdomen. The only treatment at that time was rest and a rather ineffective and totally disagreeable medication. Three weeks' recovery was not uncommon.

Murray's work was in no way hampered by impending parenthood. Classes occupied a great portion of his time. Conferences with students allowed him to encourage or offer assistance to willing students. In conferences with parents they begged him to vary slightly from the rules to permit their children to appear in a good light—especially that of receiving a passing grade in a course being failed. Only a slight change of grades would have accomplished the miracle they requested. The frequent temptation was to give in to the tearful and begging parents.

As they eagerly anticipated the birth of their first child, even the routine work like superintending the girls' dorm and dining room seemed less a chore. A set of signals had been devised by which Nova knew whether to answer "yes" or "no" to a question previously put to Murray. By one or two kicks under the table the Dicksons were always able to present a unanimous decision to all questions; the students never succeeded in playing Nova's decision against Murray's wishes. Neither could they take advantage of Nova's admitted deficiency in Spanish, which she labored to correct.

THE
GROWING
FAMILY

Fall rains took their toll before the Christmastime trip to La Paz, where Nova would await their first child's birth. Ancient adobe walls melted, and old tile roofs fell in, narrowly missing the Dicksons. Murray dispatched workmen to remove the debris for rebuilding. Before they could rebuild, another, more disastrous downpour struck. News also revealed that no rebuilding of even a roof could be done without the written permission of city government.

When Murray applied for the permit to rebuild, he was informed that they were too busy that day and he should return the next day. It was obvious that the days before leaving for La Paz would be lived in a glorified mud puddle. Floors not too smooth at best threatened to buckle completely. Even without a permit work went ahead as Murray daily visited the office to get proper authorization. Three days after the roof was completed, he no longer went for the permit, and nothing was ever heard from the "too busy official."

Murray was determined to get Nova to La Paz, where she might adjust to the high altitude before the birth of the baby. A few hours before their scheduled departure, a messenger appeared at their door with information from the police official who had issued their travel permits; he advised them to avoid travel at any cost. As he did during all his years in Bolivia, Murray went ahead with plans even in the face of delay and discomfort. Like many more trips this one would be made with the dark and ominous clouds of civil turmoil boiling overhead.

Following the tedious trip, Nova was quickly accommodated in the American clinic. In celebrating their first Christmas on the mission field, they were too bound up in the impending birth to notice how meager were their resources.

Dr. Beck had returned to the States, and Dr. Anderson assured Nova that all was well. The youngster to be born would bear a name already chosen. If it were a boy, it would be George Harkey, honoring both Murray's father and also a close friend, Jarrott Harkey. If it were a girl, the name would be Frances, honoring Nova's sister.

The tenderness of the last days of confinement was

shared so deeply that the time passed quickly. On several occasions, hearing the cries of a woman in labor, Murray left his own bed and hastened to comfort and reassure Nova. As the year 1943 died, a new life began. Frances entered the world with an abundance of curly brown hair. To the sheer delight of her father, she was active from the moment of birth.

Still suffering from the effects of new fatherhood, Murray headed back for Cochabamba to resume work. Four weeks later it was decided that Nova should fly back to the valley. After three days of waiting for improved weather, she boarded the only plane which had been able to get from La Paz to Cochabamba in a period of nearly five weeks because of the bad conditions.

Bolivians were amazed at the affection Murray demonstrated toward his new daughter. Not accustomed to such open show of affection from a father, a servant commented about it, "She is only a girl!" Murray's reply was, "Yes, but she is *my* daughter!" Another facet of the tender, love-filled personality had been cut. In letters written with extreme care so as to avoid the censor's harsh treatment, grandparents were informed of the birth, and it was obvious that Murray was proud.

January and February saw a return to familiar domestic routines. Murray even developed a large garden, necessary to the food supply for the boarding-school table. Physical labor seemed to do his spirit good, and his enthusiasm reached a high pitch as the school year began in early March. Bishop Gattinoni from Buenos Aires, in Bolivia to conduct the Methodist Annual Conference, baptized little Frances, who had established herself as queen of the household.

The Dickson home was always open to a flow of visitors. A wide range of nationalities enjoyed the hospitality of the gracious hosts. Once initiated into the Dickson home, everyone looked forward to returning to Murray's jovial stories and Nova's gracious presiding over a constantly bountiful table.

Shortly after Easter of 1944 Murray contracted typhoid fever. Nova's responsibilities trebled. She had to be extremely careful because of the baby. Murray was delirious for three weeks. During the entire period everything used in his room had to be sterilized when removed from the room. Nova's hands were terribly burned by the harsh disinfectants prescribed by the doctor. For many months she carried the scars on her hands. Still her watch and care were constant. When new antibiotics were finally secured from the United States, Murray responded. A period of six months' recuperation and regaining of strength followed.

There was much to be done. Even from his bed he both administered his section of the school work and managed to supply information for other teachers to continue his classes. As Murray recuperated, the Dicksons' friendship with the young American consul and his wife in Cochabamba blossomed. The Fourth-of-July party at the consulate was Murray's first appearance after his bout with typhoid. Years later (1964), the consul was appointed ambassador of the United States to Bolivia. A warm friendship continued through the years between Nova, Murray, and Ambassador and Mrs. Douglas Henderson.

Mail continued to frustrate Murray. One day he watched a girl steaming stamps from letters. After that he waited until the clerks hand-canceled all his letters. On one occasion he happened to hear one clerk remark to another as she rattled and smelled a box, "Oh, almonds! I'll bet the mice get into these tonight." Thereupon she tore the package open and ate.

Many letters to family strayed. Only after 1946 was it even thinkable to make remarks about the political situation, and then it still was not safe. Because of his position of leadership in The Methodist Church, Murray cultivated the habit of saving vital information for a courier who could be entrusted with letters to be dispatched upon arrival in the States. For this reason, friends often waited for many months for word from the Dicksons.

Every day was filled with the time-consuming details of classroom and administration. Late evening meals and meetings always seemed to drag with the same irritating frustration and careful attention to traditional procedure.

Late in 1944 Murray began expanding his knowledge of other Methodist work in Latin America. Elected as delegate to the Central Conference, he traveled to Buenos Aires by way of the five-day overland route. A detailed letter to his father indicated his pleasure at seeing the countryside. His work at the conference placed him in the first step of leadership among the national leaders from The Methodist Church in Argentina, Uruguay, Bolivia, Peru, Chile, Costa Rica, and Panama.

A few weeks after returning to Bolivia, Murray assumed full responsibility as director of the school. The Smiths, who had welcomed them two years earlier, departed for furlough. Mr. Smith's careful tutoring in those two years enabled Murray to assume his directorship with little problem.

Nova submitted to gynecologic surgery, then returned to Cochabamba to assist the new director in January, 1945. Murray overcame the comments about his youthful appearance with ease and established a high spirit of cooperation within the staff. His patience helped him overcome the natural resistance to an educational system controlled by the Ministry of Education, which dictated schedules, curriculum, teaching methods, even the songs to be sung in the appointed assemblies.

In the face of such conditions, not only did Murray accomplish what was expected, but the enrollment of the school reached a new peak. Along with increased revenue on which to operate came the pressures for more teaching facilities as well as more teachers.

Contacts with public officials called for supreme patience. Every process, whether civil government, educational, or social, was steeped with provincial traditionalism. Bureaucracy staggered even the patient Murray. Surmounting such tenacity to the past challenged Murray to work consistently for change.

Murray was surprised in his first visit to the Minister of Education in mid-June of 1945. He found the official well versed in the work of Murray's school, and he urged Murray to begin using English in all instruction, saying that North American teachers were the only ones who could be trusted to act unselfishly in good education of the Bolivians. He even suggested that four times as many North American teachers should be sent to aid the Bolivian education program.

During the interview, negotiations were initiated to

permit the American Institute of Cochabamba to vary from the official state program by introducing new schedules and subject materials. Considering this a monumental achievement, the Methodist leaders shortly thereafter adopted the modifications.

On the triumphant note of his interview with the Minister of Education, Murray took a group of nearly thirty youth into the jungled foothills of the Andes northeast of La Paz known as the Yungas. During the trip a number of youth were won to Christ and committed their lives to the work of The Methodist Church. Several from that group were to be prominent in the educational and church circles of Bolivia fifteen years later.

While in La Paz, Nova visited Dr. Beck, who confirmed her hope that another Dickson was on the way. With the birth anticipated for mid-February, Nova neared making good her promise to return to the States for the first furlough with two babies for family and friends to spoil.

Margaret Jane Dickson, weight seven pounds, nine ounces, arrived ahead of schedule (a rare thing in Bolivia) in La Paz on January 29, 1946. From her first breath she exhibited a healthy set of lungs. Murray and Nova reveled in the blessings of their two children as Frances somewhat roughly demonstrated her affection for the new sister.

Watching the physical development of his children and being himself aware of the rigors of work in the altitude, Murray was quick to notice the subtle changes which were worked in his fellow missionaries. Family members were also subjected to careful scrutiny. Only his own physical condition would be ignored as he became more and more involved in the life of the mission field and more and more responsibility fell to his shoulders over the years.

During a very difficult political period in 1950 the Dickson family was completed. Twice Murray traveled to La Paz to be with Nova for the birth of their third child. Each time he returned, leaving Nova in the hands of Dr. Paul Brown, who was relieving Dr. Beck. Communication via radio and telephone was primitive. On the last day of March, Murray received notice that Nova was in labor. There was no way to get to La Paz. He waited impatiently for the message the doctor promised.

After spending a frantic night, during which he played and replayed Dvorak's *New World Symphony,* drank coffee, and prayed for some word from La Paz, he started for his classes. At nine o'clock he was called to his office for a telephone call. After extended delays, during which he paced around his office, he heard Dr. Brown's voice. The conversation, overheard by many eager ears around him, went:

Murray: Paul, any news?

Paul:　　Yes. (pause)

Murray: Well?

Paul:　　It is all over.

Murray: Is it born?

Paul:　　Yes. (pause)

Murray: Is Nova all right?

Paul:　　Oh yes, Nova is fine.

Murray: What is it? (pause)

Paul:　　A boy.

Murray: A *boy!* (Again he repeated.) A *boy!*

Paul:　　A boy.

Murray's delight in having a son caused an even deeper radiance in the soft brown eyes. The entire school had heard the last exclamation of "A *boy!*" and they chorused the phrase with obvious pleasure for their beloved director.

That afternoon Murray stepped off a plane in La Paz to meet his son. Money was scarce, but this event he could not miss. Even his staff and students recognized in Murray a change from his usually mild manner to an obvious glow of pleasure.

With George Harkey Dickson's birth, Murray Dickson's family was complete. From that point on the family functioned as a team, each member contributing cause for pride on the part of every other member. It would continue until that fateful day when the clouds hung low over the mountains and in a foggy daze a drunken truck driver rounded a curve too fast on the road which hung precariously on the side of a mountain with the valley hundreds of feet below.

THE EDUCATOR
TRIES
HIS HAND

Murray undertook his responsibilities as director in a way typical of his enthusiastic thoroughness. Having taken responsibility in the midst of a school year, he guided concluding formalities, including final examination. While constantly under the pressure of administrating the school, his mind was working ahead to construction of the new building. The Smiths, who were on furlough, indicated a promise of help to build the new facility.

School administration called for travel. Murray found himself traveling to Argentina and after his delayed return, once again heading for La Paz, where buying school supplies was an on-the-spot necessity rather than something which could be trusted to written orders.

The trip to Buenos Aires was complicated when Murray discovered that his briefcase had been stolen. He lost not only business papers, but also his passport.

Sympathy was evident in the U. S. embassy where he reported loss and requested issue of a new passport; however, the law read that no new passport could be issued until the U. S. government had made a full investigation.

A new school year was about to start. Murray was desperate. Finally securing an affidavit indicating that his passport had been stolen, he appeared at the Bolivian embassy, where a kindly secretary wrote several flowery lines across the ribbon bedecked and very official-looking papers. With these in hand Murray was ready to return to Bolivia. Further complication arose, however, when an official complained that there were no fingerprints. Murray satisfied the officious bureaucrat with his delightful sense of humor and a logic too quick for the official, who dealt with only standard questions and answers. Delayed four days, Murray managed better than expected accommodations for the return trip because of a cancellation which arrived just as he purchased his tickets.

Returning with high hopes for the new year, Murray inserted a small advertisement in the newspaper indicating that "The American Institute is pleased to announce a few openings for the new school year." The response was not a flood, but the ad did stir interest, resulting in the highest registration ever attained. New teachers had to be hired, and arrangements made for duplicate use of classrooms.

Some of the students were from Roman Catholic schools which for various reasons had failed a number of students, in addition to raising the cost of tuition. With these incentives, parents persuaded Murray to enroll their children. The result was threats by priests to excommunicate parents who registered children in the Methodist school. The threat failed to dissuade very many, and the new school year opened with a rush. Murray, confessing later to overoptimism, exhibited his enthusiasm in repainting the entire school complex. In the freshened setting, instruction began.

With the European phase of World War II concluded, more interest began to filter through to mission stations in Latin America. Among the first visitors to the work of The Methodist Church in Bolivia after the war were Dr. Marshall Steel, pastor of Highland Park Methodist Church in Dallas, and Bishop Ivan Lee Holt of the St. Louis area.

Hopes were beginning to run high that work could be begun on the new school. There was no question of the need for the building. However, Murray was frustrated in all attempts to buy a vehicle to transport building materials, a process which the contractor assured him would result in great savings. He pursued all prospects for assistance by visits to the Bolivian Minister of Education and to the American ambassador. Importing firms were visited, and all materials minutely priced and repriced.

Bolivia had contributed greatly to the war. Exports of tin, rubber, and other essential raw materials returned her to the world market from which she had retreated following the Chaco War between Bolivia and Paraguay in the 1930's. Once again she looked ahead to world marketing of her commodities in face of competition.

Murray discovered a continuing struggle deeply buried within the Bolivian political scene. A sense of unity had persisted throughout the war years, but personal ambitions were returning. Political favors were being openly bought from the ruling party by people regaining an interest in politics.

Outside communication with the world was slow. Vastly improved communications media provided the masses with new ideas and gave rise to testing by groups who saw opportunity to use such innovations to their own political advantage. Radio was improving. Slanted editorials in newspapers attempted to keep readers thinking along lines which were to the advantage of newspaper persuasions.

Tensions were growing. Nighttime abductions, long

a part of the Bolivian political game of "eliminating the opposition," were increasing. In such a setting it was difficult for a school to negotiate for government help or guarantees. Still Murray labored and exuded confidence to the officials, who wondered at the energy and enthusiasm of this young director.

Errands demanding Murray's attention were countless. Purchase of a bicycle gave him much needed exercise and proved faster than the open-car trams running at snail's pace. 131427

The first taste of revolution for the Dicksons had been late in 1943. Even that had its elements of comedy. Governments seemed to rise and fall over simple issues. Those same governments seemed to make little progress in their short lives. During the 1943 escapade Murray followed the advice of older, more experienced persons and stayed off the streets.

1946 was different. With responsibility for an entire student body and nearly one hundred internas to feed, Murray made use of his knowledge of back streets in traveling to market and doing the necessary buying. On one trip he was about to be confronted by a group of self-appointed soldiers when he turned and retreated by another route.

Murray smiled, but shook his head over the pathetic humor exhibited in such scenes. One which amused him took place during the 1946 revolution. University students, always the volatile element, had called a mass meeting in the central square of La Paz. Attempting to prevent the students from regaining the sanctuary of the university buildings, the army moved quickly to encircle the university; the students stormed back toward their refuge to discover that the guards had almost completed the blockade. The illiterate and obedient soldiers of the army were still following orders when the students began fervently chanting the national anthem of Bolivia. Time and training took quick effect. Trained to stand at rigid attention whenever the national anthem was heard, the soldiers dropped their preparations, and before they knew what was happening, the entire student body of agitators swarmed past them into the sanctuary of the university buildings.

All was not quiet in Cochabamba. Stonings, looting, and even physical torture of the more detested public officials took place near the school, where Murray and family were careful to keep away from windows during periods of shooting.

Maintaining neutrality, American Institute personnel were submitted to none of the problems which engulfed other schools. Even in the strikes to bring about educational reforms and higher wages for teachers, the American Institute managed to keep relatively clear of political implications. As Murray wrote in a letter of July 27, 1946: "In the thirty-four years and dozens of revolutions through which the school has lived, its buildings have never been invaded and wrecked, and its missionaries have never been seriously threatened by mobs."

This reputation for constructive pursuits spread throughout the entire Cochabamba Valley, but Murray was plagued by larger and larger classes, less and less space to use, constant red tape preventing better education processes, shortages of books and teaching materials, and a constant financial struggle to keep the school solvent while still paying high enough salaries to attract the best available teachers. No obstacle impeded him for long before some solution was discovered, however. The school grew steadily while political and social reforms continued to ferment.

In the uncertain political and social conditions in mid-1946, Murray's influence was evidenced in the lives of the students who would assume positions of significant leadership in future years.

Asked to explain the Bolivian philosophy of life and the strange (to a North American) codes and unwritten rules of social and ethical conduct, Murray succinctly analyzed the causes for Bolivia's tragic condition in conversation with a friend: "The continent of South America is the result of conquest and settlement for profit. The reason behind all development in South America was to take profit back to Spain, or in later years to other European countries. The person who did the settling put down no roots. He exploited anyone to accumulate the wealth he sought. This was true of all mining for precious ores. It was true of the few who provided foodstuffs for troops and traders as a solid way of realizing a fortune.

"Human beings turned into slavery had no way of striking back at their conquerors but to lie, steal, and cheat. Eventually these methods became accepted as a way of life. One guilty of an offense of stealing was the object of pity that he was not smart enough to avoid getting caught. A lie was not a sin if it was expedient. Over four hundred years of Roman Catholic influence in Latin America the church avoided conflict with the powerful elements that provided it vast income at the expense of a continent of people whose very pagan virtues of honesty and personal integrity were being remolded as their only weapon against exploitation by outsiders."

Murray spoke sympathetically about the problems of the common man: "Small wages, illiteracy, and other pressures made him only too well aware that he [the national Bolivian] would be victimized by any person who had more knowledge than he had. His only defense was to retreat from even those who offered hope of changing his condition. Social consciousness and responsibility were lost in the feud between the land owner—exploiter and the peasant worker. The philosophy became a reversal of the Golden Rule. Four hundred years had made dislike, even hate, so much a part of men's distrust of one another that there was no frame of reference for love. The missionary discovered early that his was a mission to the whole man. Man's illiteracy, his physical condition, his vocational education, his education to accept new ideas were all integrated into the work which was to affect the whole man.

" 'The love of God' and the 'love of Jesus Christ' were phrases of totally foreign meaning to people who were distrusting of all newcomers whom they saw as outsiders to be avoided lest they be further cheated and exploited."

With this curt analysis Murray completed the culture shock treatment of those he introduced to the Bolivian scene. In letter after letter to friends he explained the unlimited needs in Bolivia. His arguments for such support were not only sound, but twenty years afterward the letters have a prophetic note. These prophecies became the convictions of those who worked with Murray to serve Bolivia through The Methodist Church.

One further excerpt from a letter of later date completes the background against which the years of 1946-1961 would be lived and written into history: "We have found that the improvement of mass communications of all kinds has contributed to an internal revolution in the thinking of the Bolivian people. Regularly these people see pictures and hear radio broadcasts and descriptions from politicians about the conditions of living in other countries. What they hear is beyond their imagination. Of the more essential and elemental concerns some become their ideas of what their government should provide for them. The ferment is slow, but thorough. It reaches nearly every segment of the people. 'If others can have it, why can't we?' This question has led many a local politician to make promises he could not fulfill, and cost him the next election because he could not bring about what he promised. The mutual distrust in government where his labors met with no success only spelled his downfall among his constituents."

Murray discovered friendship to be more valuable than position or legality. Money caused nearly every man to think twice about what he could or could not afford to do. Long-standing friendships with graduates would mean entry into many an office when the doors had previously been slammed in his face.

Not what you knew but who you knew often meant the difference between defeat and total success. Parents offered their personal favors or outright gifts of money and material goods for preferential treatment in the classroom or a passing grade.

Against this background of uncertain social and ethical conditions, the youthful Murray cut his teeth in administration. Well-trained teachers were hard to find. Such teachers were underpaid, and their working simultaneously in several schools to earn an adequate salary presented scheduling impossibilities. Condoning the Bolivian ethic of trading personal favor or cash for special consideration made most teachers unacceptable for teaching assignments in a Methodist mission school.

Dealing with an uncertain teacher corps added to the frustration of having to yield to directives forwarded from the Ministry of Education. Teacher strikes forced the American Institute into the awkward position of neutrality as they raised their teachers' salaries to acceptable standards.

Poverty, the existence of a social class system, political uncertainty, and other factors made the work nearly impossible at times. Unrest in the people was shown by their willingness to follow the political leader promising something better. When one is stricken with poverty, even the mere change in menu offered by a revolution has merit.

A RELATIONSHIP
to the PEOPLE
IS ESTABLISHED

Murray was never very far removed from real poverty
in his youth. He was sensitive to the problems of hard
physical work. Training in political and social sciences
made him especially observant when trends and tides
were to be watched carefully. His observations were all
the more valuable as he immersed himself in the conditions of the people and listened sympathetically to
their tales of oppression and dreams of an economy sup-
porting a vastly improved society.

The mission compound could have been a retreat
from the world, but not for Murray Dickson. Starting
with an invitation to join Rotary International, Murray
worked into positions of leadership and through the
ranks to serve as president and vice-president of the
Cochabamba club. Such civic leadership was not un-
noticed. The contacts he made not only represented the
school, but also enabled Murray to more adequately
assess the economic and social situations in the city

and nation in discussions with outstanding business-
men.

From experiences of his first term on the field, Murray wrote a friend of his concerns: "I am convinced
that my job, in fact the job of every missionary, is to
work himself out of a job. We are not here to per-
petuate the need for our being here, but to train, guide,
and so prepare the people that if we were to step out
at any time, they could carry on, not as a handicapped,
infant institution, but as the instrument for good which
we intend."

To carry out this philosophy meant being constantly
watchful for potential in students in the schools and
for men in business who could offer the church needed
leadership. Few men established in professions were
willing to gamble their status or financial security to
step into leadership in The Methodist Church. For this
reason much of the leadership to which the church
turned was young. At the same time this leadership was
energetic and would be proved during its training.

After nearly twenty years Murray emphasized the
situation: "Our best leadership has come through youth
who are not bound by traditions of 'what can't be done'
or 'how we must do it because we did it this way in
the past!' We need at least three generations to train
our own teachers and prepare our youth for positions

where the consequence of their training by the church will be felt by all of Bolivian society."

In 1960 Murray conversed with Methodist preachers and laymen permitted out of Cuba to travel in South America. These conversations stimulated his final year of work in Bolivia. He worried about a church suddenly deprived of missionary leadership. Those who worked with him became convinced that concentrating on leadership development for the church was their most important task.

The men who bear in their lives the mark of Murray's enthusiasm for their country and the evidence of his patient work with them are a monument to his tireless efforts to train adequate leadership.

In personal integrity Murray stood as tall above most men as he did physically. There might be a stern approach to a specific problem, but there was always an understanding and patient explanation of the policy determining the course. This patient teaching of principles, ethics, and moral conduct became a mark of young men and women trained under Murray Dickson. He consistently commanded their respect.

Such philosophy of absolute integrity had its humorous aspects. During the 1952 revolution Murray was forced to leave the safety of the new school to go to market for food. Using his intimate knowledge of back streets, he had almost gained his objective when a group of university students rounded a corner and confronted him with submachine guns. They were in an ugly mood resulting from lack of real direction and a desire to demonstrate their full support of revolution. The moment was exceedingly dangerous for Murray. Lining him against a wall, they were intent on executing him because he was North American; bombings of the night before had been attributed to United States' intervention in the revolution.

Feelings were running high, and the students demonstrated their fickle nature. They made one serious error: they accused Murray of being a "Yankee." This brought Murray to his fullest stature, and he replied with exaggerated dignity, "I am not a Yankee—I am a Texan." So convincing was his statement that the young rebels were sure that Murray represented something far more glorious than the United States.

As he breathed a sigh of relief, the students, some of them his former charges, began to identify themselves. They released Murray and personally guaranteed his safe conduct. Continuing his errands, he was greeted on several occasions with loud cries, "Death to the Yankees—kill the Yankees," then on spotting Murray, they would shout with glee, "Hi, Meester Deek-son!"

Training of national leadership called for unusual patience. Few ever knew how disturbed Murray became with individuals or circumstances which slowed the training of Bolivian churchmen, teachers, and administrators. Only to a few close and trusted friends would patience and understanding be abandoned to express the desire that everything would speed up. Even such expression of impatience was an indication of a commitment born of love for the Bolivian people.

Living conditions were neither simple nor easy. Periodically various ailments would drain the seemingly boundless energies of either Murray or Nova, and recuperation would be ordered. Those periods were never sufficient as both felt the need to be at work long before most people found energy to get out of bed. The whole Dickson family knew serious illness.

Shortly after birth, Margaret began bleeding profusely. Sensing the gravity of her condition, Murray called La Paz; Dr. Beck urged him to fly immediately. Reservations were nonexistent because of a recently concluded revolution. The agent for the airline suggested they appeal to the United States consulate. Several telephone calls later, arrangements were made for Nova and the baby to fly on the next flight.

When the distraught family arrived at the airport, word of the urgency had preceded them. In the rush to hold the plane, someone forgot to indicate that Frances would accompany them. The ticket agent stated emphatically but sadly that there was no room for the blonde, pig-tailed little girl. A Bolivian military wife, aware of the situation, put her arm around Frances and took her to the counter. "I forgot to tell you that I have a little girl," she said to the agent. He smiled and asked, "What is your name, little girl?" knowing well that the little blonde should be traveling with her mother and sister.

Just before the flight was announced, a very solicitous priest passed by and, when informed of the problem, said his words of blessing over Margaret. At the hospital in La Paz, Dr. Beck took over with transfusions and his usual efficient attention. Informed of the events surrounding their departure from Cochabamba and hearing of the blessing by the padre, he quipped, "Well, maybe I can save her anyway."

That touch of humor was needed in the critical situation. Three weeks of intensive care restored Margaret to serious but improving condition. Clara Graber, a nurse from Texas who had cared for Nova during several of her surgical confinements, spent long hours with Margaret. All the hospital personnel went out of their way to assist Nova and to care for Frances, who was immediately installed as queen of the clinic.

Two weeks after returning to Cochabamba with a healthy baby, Nova was stricken with acute appendicitis and forced to fly to La Paz again on an emergency basis for surgery. In these and other family crises, the Bolivians associated with the Dickson family marveled at Murray's calm efficiency; it inspired them to greater efforts in the discharge of their own tasks wherever they served men's needs.

Close friendships developed between Murray and several former students who thoroughly prepared themselves for careers within the church. Among these were Mario Salazar, son of one of the most respected educators of Bolivia, and Gaston Pol, Mario's brother-in-law. Both men shared an invaluable wealth of information and understanding of their own people which helped Murray appropriately analyze conditions and carefully plan ahead.

Bolivian leaders in The Methodist Church contributed sons and daughters to the workers' ranks. These youth threw themselves into "on the job" training. The history of Bolivian Methodism is written in the heroic lives sacrificed to see the church well founded and flourishing. Occasional scholarships enabled capable youth to study in schools in Argentina or the United States.

Murray listened and accommodated person after person. Problems, propositions, requests for favors and personal concerns were poured into the heart of one who listened receptively. Simultaneously Murray took his problems to people he knew would help if they could. Civic leaders were not only friends, but were made to feel they were potential saviors of The Methodist Church when Murray finished a long coffee-drinking session with them. People seldom failed to respond to his way of asking a favor or negotiating a business deal. His honesty effervesced; people trusted him as they would no one else.

In this trust, youth otherwise inclined discovered opportunities to serve their country with more ultimate satisfaction and result than through the frustrations of government or unstable professions which would require political alliances of dubious worth.

Slowly, through selfless devotion to people's needs, Murray won Bolivians around him to a concern for other people. A long-range view of his work granted Murray the infinite patience to confront problems head on. Exhibiting faith and patience, Murray trained his co-workers to maintain their composure as well as their faith.

Bolivians and missionaries alike faced with insurmountable problems would say with real conviction, "Just wait until Murray comes. He'll know what to do."

Murray accepted the burdens of his fellow workers as his own, whether family, work, or other concerns. Tragic news awaited him on return from one tiring trip home from the interior. Word of the accidental death of the young son of Jim and Evelyn Pace in Montero met him. Though physically exhausted, he told Nova, "They need me." Only the repair of a flat tire and restocking of the jeep with emergency rations delayed him as he left for Montero over roads where one turn could have meant tragedy to himself and his family. On his way without sleep, he arrived before actual details of the tragedy were reaching La Paz and Cochabamba. He continually extended himself physically to be where those he loved needed him.

This spirit of sharing the toils, burdens, and occasional triumphs is reflected in a letter he wrote his family in October, 1959, after a day of rough and tiring travel in the colony areas of Bolivia's southeastern jungles:

> When it was time for evening services, we preached. . . . There were four more probationary members received, and the people left to their poor huts scattered out in the tropical dark.
>
> When we reached Montero, long after ten o'clock, Katsumi and Yoshee [missionaries from the United Church of Japan who worked in the Japanese and

Okinawan colonies] and Jim and Evelyn Pace were waiting for us with cold lemonade, and we enjoyed a quiet fellowship . . . until one after another, we went off to bed, thankful for the day, burdened with the problems and tragedies of other people, grateful for the presence of God who supplies strength equal to our need.

I wish it were possible to describe the dignity and the nobility of our people here, our workers, who through smiles and tears and often with inner anguish nobly borne, struggled with and slowly conquered, go on. . . . Although I come here as a church authority . . . I am sure I always leave with a richer treasure of inspiration and dedication received from them than I am ever able to leave with them.

Men of all nations who sat with Murray Dickson seldom missed the feeling that they were in the presence of one who personified his Master. The long-range plans today being realized in Bolivia are the results of Murray's knowledge of the Bolivian mind and the potential he conceived.

Leadership is thrust upon those concerned with developing more leadership. Few who knew Murray Dickson recognized any limit to his ability. Early in 1960 Murray wrote his father of a personal battle in his conscience. Leaders of the Board of Missions had watched Murray for years. They had pointed with pride to the Bolivian work as approaching the ideal in use of personnel and resources to accomplish a maximum of good. Murray's letter reflected his personal anguish, which pressed him until his death fourteen months later: "I had a very good trip and conversation with Dr. Ellis and Dr. Smith. Both were alarmed at rumors of positions being offered me and anxious that I would go back . . . for another period, and desirous to make a place for us . . . if we did not go back to Bolivia. There are fine, new missionaries . . . but most of them are in their first terms yet, so we feel we are needed there."

Years of love and work for the people of Bolivia enabled Murray to accomplish things others could not do. Unequalled fairness in every negotiation and support of every word with principle established him as a giant in a society where so many were given to the smallness of petty pursuits and devious ways.

FINANCIAL
HARD
TIMES

Probably only while in the Wesley Foundation in Austin did Murray ever know any degree of financial freedom. In his personal concerns and work of the church Murray managed all resources with extreme caution.

Arriving on the mission field during years of extremely poor support, Murray endeavored to develop a relationship between the mission field and home churches. As late as 1960 Murray bemoaned the sacrifices of missionary families. "Look at _____ and _____! They are putting half their income into building that church because they believe it necessary. And to think that we had to turn down their request for a grant from general funds." Though he and his family had often set the example, Murray never ceased to marvel at others' sacrifices.

Meticulous attention to detail resulted in heroic use of money which arrived on the mission field. In tribute to Murray's administration a U. S. government official remarked to a visitor, "With men like Murray Dickson managing the work of The Methodist Church in Bolivia, they get twenty times as much result from a dollar as we get."

Respect for Murray's administrative ability and knowledge of Bolivia's needs prompted foreign-aid officials to rely heavily on Murray's insights. Separation of church and state was a moot question when technical personnel and equipment could be interchanged with mutual respect to provide benefit to Bolivians.

Financial distresses in 1945 finally led to orders to sell the American Institute in La Paz, mother institution of Bolivian Methodism. In a letter bordering on panic, Murray wrote Dr. M. O. Williams at the Board of Missions in New York on April 25, 1945: "The Methodist Church has a terrific responsibility . . . it is within our power to change the course of history in these countries of Latin America—*if we don't make the mistake of too little and too late!* The danger is that in the justifiable interest and emphasis on reconstruction in the war-torn countries of Europe and the Orient, we are apt to overlook the less spectacular work in these neighboring countries which are also in crisis, a crisis more serious because more subtle, more dangerous because the forces at work in them are surreptitious and less obvious in their operation."

This impassioned plea to Dr. Williams was repeated in countless letters to everyone upon whom Murray could place the claim of Christian friendship. His anxieties were underscored by his dreams of what could result from continued and enlarged work of The Methodist Church: "If you could hear in person the testimony of the liberals in any Latin American country about the power and force of our mission schools in the struggle for democracy, if you could see firsthand the work of some of the dictatorships they oppose— then indeed you could understand what is at stake. In Bolivia almost all the genuinely progressive leaders in the last twenty years have been students in our mission schools. . . . Now we have lost our school in La Paz for lack of support from the Board of Missions and from churches in the States. Our only hope is to maintain and expand the work of the school here in Cochabamba. We have to have more American teachers to do it!"

The La Paz school was at last saved through expedient action by friends, was restored to financial solvency, and then marked by amazing growth.

Few who heard or read Murray's straightforward statements of need and the accompanying opportunity failed to respond. Money did not exactly flood in, but from the time Murray arrived on the field, interest in Bolivia increased steadily. Even his death marked an acceleration in support from friends of Murray.

In 1946 when money was so short, new property waited to be used. Increasing enrollment in hazardous and antiquated facilities took dedication and concentrated administration. Such dedication was a far cry from the ideas which Murray had espoused ten years before. He confessed this in a letter to a Texas Methodist Student Conference meeting in Hillsboro, Texas:

> Now we are missionaries. It hasn't been long since, as a student at S.M.U., I was strongly opposed to missions. I remember having made a speech . . . against the idea of taking a collection for a visiting missionary on the basis there was plenty to be done in Dallas. . . . My concept of a missionary was of an elderly person dressed in a funny costume who put on a display in the local church to tell sob stories to raise money to save the poor heathen.

> Now I am a missionary. Not that kind . . . I have learned that missions mean agriculture, medicine, engineering, education as well as preaching . . . that there is a need for missionaries of all kinds, with all types of preparation. I want to tell you about that need. Nova and I have been here four years now, and we have some idea of what it is all

about. To begin with, don't let anybody get you to the mission field on the basis of heroics. Missionary work doesn't seem heroic to us, at times it comes closer to being a grind. There are all sorts of inconveniences. We live at school . . . to take care of the boy's dormitory. We are on call twenty-four hours a day. The food is poor, at times even unpleasant. There is no privacy at all. . . . The roof leaks, and the stove smokes. Occasionally we get on the nerves of fellow missionaries and they on ours.

Working at this altitude we suffer subtle breakdown of nervous reserves without quite understanding what is going on. There is nothing heroic about this business. It's just a matter of keeping on. Yet we wouldn't trade this for anything else in the world.

Those who observed the young, lithe Texan with the soft and twinkling eyes smiled to themselves as they followed his efforts to balance the budget in the school. Nearly every order was submitted for personal checking; every expenditure was to be justified. Much of the buying in the local market to supply the school dormitories was done by Murray.

The first few trips to the market caused an uproar. Men just did not buy in the market. Women vendors of fruits and vegetables and sparsely stocked piles of canned goods made the most of this man who did a woman's work.

They discovered quickly that Murray was a sharp bargainer. More often than not Murray won in the sport of friendly haggling over price. A day-to-day running battle often won Murray some prized object which he wanted for the school or as a surprise for his beloved Nova. Only by careful buying could he afford to give such extravagant gifts as a bar of stateside soap or other seemingly insignificant remembrance. Everyone in the market knew Murray was completely crazy the day he began to bargain for a native costume. His obvious uneasiness created a hearty laugh about the "gringo" who bought Indian clothes for his wife.

One incident is related in a letter of July, 1944: "I don't think I have told you about Frances' basket. I hunted until I found what I wanted. The woman asked forty bolivianos for it, but after haggling, she sold it for thirty. . . . I shopped for some fruit and ended up near where I had bought the basket. All of a sudden there was a shrill screech and someone grabbed my basket. . . . It was the basket woman. She said that thirty bills was not enough. I insisted that the sale had been made, at which she screamed the more. There we stood in the middle of the market, she pulling on one handle, me pulling on the other. I finally made her give me my money back and let her have the basket, whereupon she took it back to her stall and hid it under all the others. A week later I went back to the market, and there was the basket. She started at forty and came down to thirty-two. I told her thirty was my last price, so she sold it to me for thirty, and I hurried away before she could change her mind again."

By marketing Murray gained insight into the lives of the common people. It also caused him to shake his head and wonder how the common man could live where commodities were so costly. This added dimension placed Murray in a position to appreciate the difficulties of the people The Methodist Church served.

Family finances also demanded careful attention. Birthday, anniversary, and Christmas gifts which arrived from the States in the form of checks were always opportune. Usually money was deposited in a stateside account, not entrusted to the unreliable mails. Occasionally when things seemed most difficult, an unexpected gift would arrive and permit Murray either to meet family expenses, if the gift were for family use, or to meet some obligation of the school and church, if it were for mission work.

Such providential gifts became too frequent to dismiss lightly. Although Murray maintained a faith that was unshakable, he could never hold to himself his amazement at the fortunes which befell his family and the mission just when it seemed that drastic action would be necessary.

In this strained setting a new church was started; it was not without sacrifice. Moises Merubia, a Cochabambino, had been educated in the United States at Garrett Theological Seminary. On his return to Bolivia to work, he and his wife refused any salary, insisting rather that the money be set aside for a new church. With such devotion and the sacrificial giving of the stalwart Bolivians who worshiped and studied under the Merubias, the church began its building.

Just before Christmas, 1946, a cablegram arrived from New York authorizing construction of the new school building. Then real financial struggle began. There is a Bolivian idiom having the same meaning as the American saying, "There is more than one way to skin a cat." Between Murray Dickson and LeGrande Smith every possible avenue of saving or expediting construction was explored. Every hint of substituting better materials was investigated.

Murray and Mr. Smith chose this situation to educate the Bolivian people to support the schools where their children studied. Projects of all sorts were initiated to enable many persons to take pride in the accomplishment of building the new school.

Desirable materials were in short supply. Workmen had to be watched like hawks, lest their ancient ways of theft strip the project of badly needed materials. Each batch of cement, each section of floor had to be carefully inspected to assure proper ingredients. Supervision was necessary; progress was slow.

As construction slowly progressed, Murray and Nova faced their first furlough. Neither would consent to leave Mr. Smith with the burdens of construction supervision and administering the school by himself. A search was instigated for missionaries to arrive in time to relieve some of the heavy work load. Money was at the core of the problem; funds were not being showered upon the Bolivian work of The Methodist Church.

Bolivians who worked in the school and church marveled constantly at the personal integrity of Methodist mission personnel. Clear and exact records, correct to the last Boliviano, were demanded by Murray and Mr. Smith.

Gifts of any kind were a sacred trust to Murray, and he never permitted delay in seeing that the gift was recognized and dispatched immediately toward its intended purpose. Murray's delightful thank-you letters contained accounts of the work and opened the door for further financial support.

Expansion of the mission work was never an excuse

for lessening the careful stewardship which Murray accepted as his trust. As his responsibilities became greater in positions of administration to which he was called, his devotion to that careful stewardship only increased.

Murray could not wait until he got home to tell the story and try his hand at interesting his Methodist friends in increased support for the work in Bolivia. At this he was to become a master.

Furloughs became opportunities to crusade for new understanding and support of Christian missions. Armed with facts and filled with stories of his four years, Murray eagerly anticipated his first furlough.

FURLOUGHS
ARE
for REST?

"The happiest news we have had in some time is that it looks as if we shall soon have reinforcements," commented Murray in a letter to his parents. Anticipation of their first furlough was sharpened with the promise of new missionary personnel to whom they could entrust the work they had been doing.

In voluminous correspondence Murray had indicated that they would stay on the field for an extra year. This note of sincere sacrifice and willingness to put aside personal desires underlay their honest concern to remain where the work was so heavy.

With help on the way, the preparations began for the furlough. The first term had taken its toll. Nova had had two babies and submitted to surgery three times. Murray had worked long and hard, often while suffering from one of the local infections. His siege of typhoid had left him weak and slow in recovering.

Most important, Murray could not wait to report

what he had found in Bolivia. He knew that the answer
to much of his concern for Bolivia lay in cultivation of
churches for support. In this way the furlough was
anticipated more than ever.

A practical approach to furlough was dictated as
Nova and the children departed early to allow Nova
to receive medical attention. Left alone, Murray spent
the little extra time in the necessary, favorite pastime
of gardening. He shared in the cornerstone-laying for
the new school before he departed. By then he could
report the specific needs for the new building.

Nova no more than reached home than her correspondence was filled with details of people wanting to
schedule Murray for appearances before groups of all
kinds. The list was nearly complete before Murray arrived for Christmas of 1947.

Every day was filled with appearances before groups
hungry to hear Murray's vivid descriptions of life in
the faraway mountain valley of Cochabamba. He had a
flair for details; his word pictures made the mission
field live. Some persons questioned his stories because
they were nearly unbelievable. Still the persuasive enthusiasm of the missionary fresh from the field was
contagious. His fame spread, and the schedule
tightened.

Submitting to the required Board of Missions'

physical examination, Murray reported a skinny 150 pounds on his six-foot frame. In spite of an exhausting schedule, the furlough year restored him to excellent physical condition and 175 pounds.

A second requirement was that part of the furlough be used for postgraduate or advanced study. Murray selected Columbia University for study of practical as well as theoretical courses.

Every break in the school schedule saw Murray traveling to churches to tell his story of Bolivia. Well aware of the interest which could be created by the use of colored slides, Murray sought to illustrate all his stories with vivid words and sharp pictures. Every weekend he traveled, often returning late Sunday night for Monday classes. He drank in every bit of material offered in the classroom and found in library research and reading.

Each furlough multiplied the number of churches exposed to Murray's winsome presentation until it became impossible to meet all requests for appearances. Even then his friendly letters reflected the warmth of the man who made missions live and become personally important to everyone who heard him.

Murray's letters were so valued that friends thoughtlessly accused him of being a poor correspondent. Little did they imagine the volume of his correspondence.

Friends coveted the personal touch with missions maintained in the vivid letters. In each letter Murray tried to include some description of an event or illustration which could be passed on in the group represented by the correspondent. These tidbits from the mission field kept interest high and very personal.

Near the end of the first furlough Murray spoke in Boston Avenue Methodist Church in Tulsa, Oklahoma. The pastor was Dr. H. Bascomb Watts, father of Murray's friend of S.M.U. days, Ewart Watts. Murray's presentation of the cause of Bolivia was so moving that a typical problem arose. Dr. Watts took Murray aside and invited him to join the ministerial staff of the great Tulsa church. He had recognized Murray's contagious wholesomeness and wanted to put it to work in his church.

Murray's reaction was an admission of mixed emotions. There was honor in the invitation, but Bolivia called, and Murray politely declined. In the following days Dr. Watts renewed the invitation, but Murray remained loyal to Bolivia. Completely captivated by Murray's enthusiasm and purpose, Dr. Watts spoke directly to him, "If I can't have you one way, I will get you another. From now on, Boston Avenue will provide your support in the mission field."

With a great church behind them and new friends

constantly being added to the list of those interested in their work, Nova and Murray faced return to the field with renewed spirit. The end of the furlough year was in sight. Increasing numbers of new and old friends promised to support their work. The young man who had years before so heartily opposed missions had become a very strong voice in their support and interpretation. That same man, who had felt that he was "not good enough to become a minister of the gospel," was informed by Southwest Texas Conference Methodists that he had met the requirements for ordination and had been elected to that office. Another step in his journey was firmly taken.

Furloughs became a kind of "mission" in themselves. Murray never underestimated the potential of any church where he appeared to stir the imagination as to what gifts to the mission field would mean. On the field Murray would occasionally yield to the temptation to express his inner thoughts about the complacency and lack of understanding of church people in the United States. His thesis was: "They simply don't know! If only they could see it, smell it, and live with it for a few hours, our work would be different. We would have problems putting everything they provided to honest work."

In addition furloughs became crusades to enlighten

Methodists in the United States. Murray's theme description was: "We have built false walls or barriers to knowing our brother's condition. The early church grew because of men who took the gospel to a specific group and applied it. Those who went returned to tell of the successes, and their supporters were as thrilled as the missionaries. We must recapture those joys shared between workers in the field and the providers at home."

So effective was Murray's interpretation of Bolivia that many substantial objectors to missions experienced what Murray had known in changing concepts. Hundreds of people came to participate in a new aspect of their Christian faith because of the ongoing, warm, and enthusiastic personality of Murray.

Texas was not always fertile soil for mission cultivation. Some men of wealth, inclined to isolation and extreme conservatism, were quick to challenge Murray. The early days of debate training made Murray's statements clear and concise. His alert and agile mind fielded questions and not only shot back accounts of personal experience, but also backed up the ideas with statistics.

From the favored position of "having been there" Murray spoke of things that men inclined to ignore missions could not always accept. He challenged these men to either go and see for themselves or else cease objecting to a church which reached beyond the confines of its own walls.

Bolivia was not the only recipient of support as the result of Murray's appearances. Leaders from many mission fields attributed renewed support for their projects to his interpretation of Christian missions.

Ideas began to take shape during furloughs. Murray saw the improvements in communications and also especially in rapid and safe air transportation. When he met men involved in mass media, he was quick to inquire how the new advances could be applied to the mission field. These advances he used as basis for plans to interpret what was happening in the field to the home churches and to improve the teaching and other programs of the mission field. Radio occupied much of Murray's interest; he knew what the increased use of radio could mean. As early as 1947 he talked at length with executives and companies to ascertain costs, equipment requirements, and technical help necessary for the church to put radio to fruitful use.

Furloughs were always too short. If any part of a furlough was neglected, it was time with the family. Although it meant time away from the field, it was another kind of demanding work. For many, furloughs were more taxing than a year on the mission field.

Murray thrived on the demanding schedule of appearances and periods of travel. He utilized every available method from rented cars to flying in private aircraft. Men who provided and piloted their private planes exhibited the same eagerness with which everyone sought to share Murray's company. They felt they had spent time not in serving but in being served. No period of travel with Murray Dickson was common; there was always some new world to be explored, some new subject which pertained to living the Christian life and its demands to be investigated.

Murray used ingenious ways of providing insights into Christian living for those who accompanied him. Those who spent a few minutes or long hours with him were richer for the privilege. His reputation of exuding confidence and the joy of the Christian gospel gave Murray a degree of fame throughout the United States. He was in early demand for a wide variety of world mission conferences. His concepts of mission work were such that he was selected by the Board of Missions to give the featured presentation of the quadrennial report to the 1960 session of the General Conference of The Methodist Church, which met in Denver. Even in that setting of such importance, Murray struck such a note of contagious personal warmth that results continued long after the conference.

Furloughs are for rest? They never were for Murray

Dickson, who managed to turn each furlough into a work session producing perhaps greater results in the United States than in his work in the mission field in Bolivia. Furloughs were a change of scene, but even more of a challenge than he found on the field.

His words in 1961 after returning to the field were significant: "Something is wrong at home. People are complacent. They want to be left alone. They only hear half of what you say and tell them. They don't believe or don't want to believe that there is another side to life. Our mission is now doubled, since we not only have the work to occupy us in the field, but we have to wake up the church at home!"

Occasional emergency trips on business to the United States permitted appearances at churches where extra interpretation of the mission work always resulted in increased support. Murray never missed an opportunity to interpret Bolivia to anyone who would listen.

THE
ROOTS
GROW DEEPER

During infrequent moments alone before returning to
Bolivia from their first furlough, Nova and Murray
spoke of their concrn about their new assignment.
Cochabamba had been their home, but mission-field
assignments sent personnel where they were needed
most. Murray wanted badly to return to the school
under construction and to shoulder some of the growing responsibility.

Delight was more than apparent when they were re-
assigned to Cochabamba. On arrival they discovered
little change and much remaining to be done. Within a
day they entered into full schedules of work in preparation for the new school year.

Murray assumed personal responsibility for overseeing the school construction. Whether or not it was his
appointed task was a moot question. He watched every
minute detail in the tedious process of antiquated
Bolivian methods of construction.

With resources gathered while on furlough, Murray was able to lighten the financial burden slightly. Even this extra was insufficient. The old property on Plaza Colon had to be sold. Several offers had been received, and those were pursued. After long hours tendering social graces, one of the offers was found to be satisfactory. Sale was negotiated, and the final piece in the financial puzzle fitted into place.

Barely was this completed when political storm clouds broke with alarming speed over the serene valley. In a period of less than three weeks a revolution was begun, fought, and concluded. The scene continued to be tense. Skeptical Cochabambinos walked carefully and caste furtive glances around them. Schools dared not open because of the unrest.

Once the unrest subsided and school began, Murray was at his familiar post as principal. His teaching load was heavy. The administrative load was complicated with the unending problems of bureaucracy. Progress on the new building was slow but steady; each inspection revealed some small advance. Murray became a familiar figure as each evening he bicycled to the site and with practiced eye examined the work.

Routine was almost established when word arrived that Murray had been selected to head a missions conference in Connecticut. His mind slipped into high gear as he anticipated the time when he could "sell" the mission field in Bolivia to the very select fifty couples who would attend the conference at Hartford the following summer.

School, church, and other activities demanded long hours of detail work. With lectures to prepare, papers to grade, and other demands felt, none of the romance of the mission field was evident. The detail work was necessary for good education, and Murray was completely faithful to the task.

Winter months were drawing to a close in 1949 when unrest again hit Bolivia. For several days things were so tense that only excerpts from Murray's letter of September 8, 1949, to his parents can describe it:

> When we started to town . . . we found . . . that the main square was blocked off. The MNR [Movimiento Nacional Revolucionario] had pulled a coup d'état and were in power. . . . We skirted the main part of town and entered the market from another direction. We were half through buying when a number of people came running through the marketplace shouting. In a matter of seconds the Indians were gathering up their merchandise, folding up their produce and disappearing. . . . By the time we could gather all our helpers, the excitement had apparently abated, but half the vendors had gone. We continued buying food . . . and

finally started for the school . . . only about three blocks from the center of the city. Just as we stopped . . . the firing began. We could see people shoot and fall on the corner ahead of us . . . I was scared. But the dormitory had to have food so one of the peons and I unloaded food in the doorway while Mrs. Smith, Mrs. Salazar, and a visiting teacher . . . lay on the floor of the station wagon. As quickly as we could, we raced backwards up a one-way street . . . went the wrong way on another to the high school where the boys' dorm is. There was firing in that neighborhood too. We hurried on out to the new school. Fortunately all is quiet on our side of the river. . . . We are glad that in selecting the site we chose one far from all military objectives.

All afternoon we heard machine gun fire and heavier fire which we later learned was dynamite explosions.

Then came airplanes over the city dropping leaflets and warning that the city would be bombed if the revolutionaries did not give up. . . . Just as a new flight of planes came over . . . we decided to evacuate the two dormitories near the center of town . . . so I lit out in the station wagon. It took five trips, and again I was scared.

Departing from the story, Murray related that in the midst of the confusion a woman who had done much harm to the school by promoting troubles with the priests called and said that her baby was being born, but the priests would not take her to the hospital. Murray relented and raced her to the clinic, driving through dangerous areas where firing was heavy.

When we finally got all the dormitory students out to the new school . . . we felt a little better. Betty and Bill Holt stayed at the school. . . . Firing was sporadic all night. . . . Toward morning . . . we were getting some good sleep when the first bomb dropped. I ran out of doors. . . . I could hear planes and see flashes. . . . I stood there dazed for some minutes. . . . Then I remembered Bill and Betty. Running to the station wagon . . . I headed for town, running without lights . . . speeding down the main street with only the starlight and bomb flashes to guide me. And I was scared again. My throat felt dry and parched, and I felt numb all over. By the time Betty, Bill, and the baby were in the car, there was smoke and a glare from the huge fire. . . . The gasoline deposits at the airport had been hit. We hurried back to the new school . . . away from the center of town.

[Later that Sunday morning Bill and Murray went into town to open the church for services. The central plaza was a shambles from the fighting. After services they returned to the school across the river from the center of town.]

141

We had just finished lunch when the bombing started again. We ran to a spot on the mountainside above the school. . . . Bill had a good pair of field glasses, and we could see the thing with horrible clarity. There was no antiaircraft fire, so the bombers were flying rather low. They made run after run across the airport and the military base nearby. . . . Then one of the planes circled directly over where we were and leveled off over the city itself. I watched through the glasses. The red tile roofs, the rounded cupolas, the church towers, the trees among the houses all seemed so beautiful. . . . Surely no Bolivian could bomb this.

Suddenly a tremendous explosion and another and another, and the peaceful panorama sprouted angry billowing clouds, and the thunder of explosions shook us. Numbed, almost paralyzed, we stood and watched. Another run over the airport and the bombers left. . . . When the planes had gone, Bill and I went downtown to see about the schools. . . . Two bombs had fallen in police offices which were in the hands of revolutionaries and their leaders. Friends who came to warn us indicated that the revolutionaries who had seized the radios and telephone system . . . had announced that the bombing had been done by American planes. . . . We went back to the school.

Murray reported that the next day he and Lloyd Middleton went into the schools and removed valuable papers, mattresses, and office equipment before the mobs attacked. He heard the story of the foiling of the plan to take over the central bank: "The bank president had been too smart for them. He had divided up all the money among the directors, who had taken it off and hidden it, and he had gone off to the country place . . . with the keys. When the rebels finally found him and forced him . . . to open the vaults, they found only about BS 1,200 or U.S. $12."

A vivid paragraph described another narrow escape when Murray and Lloyd were confronted by submachine gun-carrying men who were confiscating vehicles, By fast driving over back streets, Murray evaded capture, and they regained the peaceful side of the river. "That afternoon I walked into town to do pastoral visiting—a family whose youngest child had died, shot through the lung . . . and two other families who had especially nervous members."

Murray's account then recalled the Tuesday on which the Holts returned to school only to hear a Wednesday-morning rumor that government troops would attack and there would be a fierce battle. Another rush trip evacuated the Holts and students again.

Before daylight the next morning firing began: machine guns, rifles, artillery. . . . We climbed the

hill . . . but the valley was so filled with smoke we
could make out very little. . . . Bill and I decided
to go to town since I was afraid the family [of the
young child who had been shot] would try to go to
the church for memorial services. . . . But when we
got to the footbridge we found it guarded by
government troops. . . . The two bridges above and
below were also in the hands of troops. . . . I asked
permission to cross and was refused, so we with-
drew . . . and waited. After quite some time we tried
again, and this time they let us across. We hurried
and reached there just as the family was leaving to
go to the church. By noon it was all over. . . . During these days we have had much to be thankful
for. No member of our staff nor student of ours was
injured. We are thankful to God.

The longer Murray worked in Bolivia the more he
was able to think like a Bolivian. Several of their
customs he found delightful and so adopted them. The
Bolivians noted and appreciated this. One of the happiest discoveries Murray made was the poncho. Not
long after arriving in Bolivia, he found a woman who
would weave a poncho big enough to fit him. When
asked what color, Murray replied with gusto, "Why
red, of course!" He wore the poncho faithfully; hikes
into the mountains around Cochabamba meant that the
poncho was a part of the clothing he wore. After only

a few years he was known in the valley as "el gringo en el poncho rojo" [the gringo in the red poncho]. Several times during travels when stopped at road-blocks manned by drunken Indians, he was recognized by the red poncho and permitted to proceed.

Another part of his traveling gear he nearly missed getting. From the moment he decided he needed the boots until they were finally on his feet, a struggle ensued. He used considerable persuasion to get his order mailed. By a quirk of fate the boots lay misplaced in customs in Panama for six months. When they did arrive in Bolivia, little quarreling was done over the customs fee. After all, who in Bolivia could wear size 11D! That fact alone accounted for the notification that the boots had arrived instead of having been stolen in customs.

The little customs official looked at the man who was big like a "Yanqui," but whose eyes were warm like a Bolivian's. "Here are your boots, Señor. That will be a small fee. Only ten American dollars, Señor."

Murray was quick. "What? Ten dollars? Why how outrageous! Take them. Send them back! Ten dollars?"

"Oh, Señor, but the boots are new."

"They have been on their way for ten months. I had to wear shoes up to Tunari. Plain shoes walking up

Tunari. Do you realize how my feet hurt, how cold my feet got?"

"You walked up Tunari?"

"Yes, and it was a hard walk without these boots. Send them back!"

"Only two dollars, Señor. Thank you. Tell me, Señor, is it pretty up there? How is it? They tell me the condor lives up there."

Climbing Tunari was considered a feat of some physical fortitude. And the customs man was duly impressed as well as influenced by the insistence that the boots be returned, which would have meant much work for him.

The boots and poncho were symbolic of the travel Murray did continually throughout Bolivia. As his leadership was recognized, travel took him away from home more and more. Much of the time he traveled in the red poncho and big boots.

No travel was easy, and much of Murray's was beyond the beaten path where roads were not reliable. A four-wheel-drive vehicle was mandatory. Murray wore out at least six; he drove his vehicles as mercilessly as he did himself.

Careful preparations were as necessary as skillful driving. Tools included tire pumps and equipment, patches, spare parts, extra oil, grease gun, extra gas and water, and the ever-helpful pick and shovel. A well-prepared vehicle made the driver quite self-sufficient. Spare cans of food were always included in case he was stranded for extended periods. An extra tarpaulin or ground cloth served not only to hide his collection of desirable tools, but occasionally was pressed into action for other varied uses.

When appointed district superintendent in his second term on the field, Murray began travel in earnest. As he traveled, he became more convinced that plans had to be made for extending the work of the church into the interior of Bolivia. During this period the U. S. government began its first substantial aid programs assisting the Bolivians in road construction and general improvement of transportation. Long before survey teams recommended routes, Murray had either driven a treacherous trail or had walked the distance to meet village leaders in remote places.

In such conditions everyone who traveled was a companion. There is no way of knowing how many fortunate persons accepted the rides Murray offered in desolate areas. In the face of problems and adverse road conditions, Murray's shoulder was the first to be set to the wheel. He was always ready to help someone in need, remembering that often he had been helped.

Wilson Boots, a youthful missionary in his days in

Bolivia, offered tribute to Murray in a story he told in a letter of condolence to the Dickson children following Murray's death:

> For several of us one of the most memorable experiences with your father was in 1955 . . . on an extensive trip through the interior of Bolivia. We had arrived . . . at a river which had risen considerably due to rains upstream. It seemed impossible to ford. A number of trucks were waiting on both sides . . . for the water to lower to permit passage. After waiting a number of hours, we decided that the water had gone down enough so we could cross. . . . We drove across, but just barely made it. The stream was so swift and high that the water came into the jeep and soaked our luggage. We realized how fortunate we had been . . . and were very firm in telling three other young men in the jeep behind us that they should not try it. . . . However they went ahead . . . and immediately became stalled in midstream. They were in a dangerous situation, since the current was about to carry them and the jeep tumbling downstream. They needed help immediately, but none of the thirty or forty truck drivers . . . had the courage to do anything. Your father [Murray] was the only one with the courage to act.
>
> He grabbed a chain from one of the trucks and went down into the deepest and swiftest part of

the water to fasten the chain . . . and worked in the water while directing a truck on how to pull the jeep out. It was a dramatic demonstration of a characteristic which distinguished your father in all aspects of life—his willingness to sacrifice himself in the service of others. The New Testament which I use for daily devotionals still carries the soiled, vivid reminder of your father's example and of the obedience to the cross in the service of others demanded of every Christian.

Wilson Boots put into words what others discovered when they met Murray. There was about him a gentleness which made people trust him even in the most adverse conditions. Coupled with that gentle confidence was the nobility of a convinced leader whose command was sure and steady. That characteristic needed no explanations for Bolivians who were illiterate and lived removed from the rush of commerce and mass media. Murray won the love of these people through the confidence he radiated and his very evident concern for their condition.

Quietly humble but with a thorough knowledge of his own potential, he drew strength from a source his working companions had not tapped. In addition a sense of humor enabled Murray to disregard his own efforts and give others the credit for all accomplishments.

Murray loved to tell of Jack Robison's encounter with the village elders who appeared one morning and asked Jack to begin a school for them. Jack methodically explained that the community would have to provide certain help. He promised that he would travel to the village in a few days and lay plans with them. The next morning the same group reappeared with the news that they had cast several hundred adobe bricks and that an affluent man in the community had given land for the school. They were ready for action. Jack told them he needed time to find a teacher and to secure supplies.

The third day the group returned and announced an astounding number of adobes ready for building. The entire community would also become Methodist as soon as the school was built. As the group left the mission compound, they were confronted by the area priest who inquired the nature of their business. Proudly the leader spoke of the impending school. With a flourish he also promised a new church and added the coup d'état: as soon as they completed the church, they would tear down the ancient Roman Catholic chapel in the village.

In humorously relating such stories, Murray drew vivid illustrations of the potential awaiting The Methodist Church in Bolivia. Knowing this potential, Murray drove himself relentlessly. He became a human dynomo, unable to hold himself to a single task; his mind raced ahead of others laying plans, sketching out details, and exercising leadership for a substantial church founded on the principle of serving the needs of the whole man.

Every new village he entered or heard about, every new Bolivian he met made his resolution more firm. He was totally committed to serving the total needs of a whole nation.

Not all was high and visionary planning, however. Murray enjoyed life and made the most of moments of adventure and relaxation. It took a man of some coolness and courage to hunt alligators from a dugout canoe with shotgun and flashlight. Murray was hunter enough to realize the danger, yet sport enough to appreciate that either he shot well at the diamond-bright eyes in the dark, or he would be in serious difficulty with a wounded alligator turning over the canoe with one swipe of its huge tail. This excitement added to Murray's enthusiasm for the infrequent evenings when he managed to escape and pursue some challenging sport. Hours for relaxation were far too few.

Nothing seemed to hinder the activity of the man. With construction nearing completion on the new high school, one evening Murray took one misstep and fell hard to the ground, fracturing his leg. As the doctor worked on the awkward cast, he was asked if Murray would ever climb Tunari again. Knowing the break to be serious, the doctor replied that it was doubtful. Less than six months later Murray again stood atop the majestic mountain. A slight limp remained, apparent only to those who knew to look for it.

The cast was a nuisance; it slowed Murray down slightly. Those working with him carried out his instructions and took their problems to him; they relied on him in confinement as they had when he was at his desk. He missed only one Sunday, then secured a special stool on which he sat to preach in the little church where, in addition to his other duties, he was pastor.

Anxious moments were a part of life as Murray lived it; he was human. When unsuccessful in persuading others, he never knew what to expect, but in every situation the Bolivians saw the same side of the man— his absolute adherence to honesty and a conviction of confidence.

It is little wonder that a wife who shared such uncertainty, such conviction, and such an attitude of service would not only insist that the mortal remains of such a spirit be buried in Bolivian soil, but would herself retrain to better serve Bolivia as she returned to work there.

THE POWER of FAITH
and the
VICTORY of SACRIFICE

After eleven years on the mission field, Murray wrote a letter which was widely circulated among his friends. The letter portrayed the change that had been worked in the life of one who debated Christian missions from the negative side while in college. Some of it was classic in its expression of the philosophy of Christian missions:

> We learned the first important lesson for our missionary career: Christianity is a religion for crisis, and it works. That lesson has stood us in good stead all the way.

> In Cochabamba . . . we began to learn other lessons. Our room was an empty, dismal place furnished with an ancient bed that collapsed when we sat on it. . . . There was no sofa, no easy chair . . . no kitchen. . . . We were to eat the greasy, highly seasoned food prepared by the Indian cook for Indian tastes. The bath was out through the main

patio, up a flight of stairs, along a balcony in front
of the classrooms, through a hall, and back on the
far wing. . . . During the first year, as we struggled
to accustom ourselves to the food and altitude, we
christened this trek, "the hundred-yard dash."

But we were no worse off . . . than the rest. . . . No
missionaries of our church . . . lived in houses. . . .
We occupied unused rooms in schools or in the
hospital.

In the third paragraph of his letter Murray went on
to give a concise historical account of the slow growth
of The Methodist Church in Bolivia. Facts and analysis
presented a dreary picture. He confessed:

We were discouraged and homesick. Even more
poignant than the apparent failure of the work
were our difficulties with language and adjust-
ments to strange living conditions. Then one day
the elderly Bolivian pastor came to see us. He
wanted us to be treasurers of the fund he was
starting to build a new church. . . . We thought
the old man was crazy. How could fifteen poor
members in a community where even visiting the
Protestant church might cost a man his job build
a church? But when I protested, the old man
smiled, "Son, God will provide." He left a generous
contribution to start the fund. After that he
regularly turned back his own small salary . . . to

apply to the fund. Others began to catch his faith and determination. He died soon afterward, but two years from the date of his death we laid the cornerstone and began the slow process of building. These miserably poor people themselves raised half the cost of it, and after they got the unfinished walls crowned with a roof, before they had ceiling or floor, or glass in the windows, they doubled their giving to the Indian work in Ancoraimes, which was poorer than we were. As the church went on to completion, we learned the second important lesson: *the power of faith and the victory of sacrifice.*

The letter suddenly came alive with optimism and reports of new work and success. Help from Argentina and Uruguay in additional personnel stimulated all work. Financial help began to arrive to answer the most pressing needs. Murray carefully credited each person and church that had provided crucial help, on which new and substantial progress depended. Objective review now provides a more realistic picture of what Murray was writing about. He had played a large part in the progress he described, but typical of his humility he would claim no credit.

Murray's philosophy of Christian missionary work was colored by his own relationship to the church and especially undergirded by his personal faith. Everyone who shared his stories and heard his analysis of the potential for the church in Bolivia caught some of his enthusiasm. To hear Murray speak about his adopted country was to be exposed to a contagion which would never leave a person free to be selfish or detached from the universal mission of the church.

The mission was Murray—Murray was the mission. At every turn he encountered inconsistency born of distrust; inadequacy born of ignorance; lack of ethical practice born of years of exploitation of neighbors; and the tragedy of a country filled with illiteracy, poverty, disease, and geographical handicaps. A further concern haunted Murray. He met people who had absolutely no social conscience; even their patriotism was blindly shouted rather than firmly grasped.

Where to begin? Murray believed that the Christian mission involved serving the whole man. He failed to see how anyone could preach the love of God to a man whose stomach was empty, children illiterate, and wife filled with disease. Murray was practical to the point of involving himself in any plan or program which would enable the common people to better themselves in honorable ways and to gain self-respect. To this end Murray allied himself with any agency working with people.

U. S. government officials continued to value Murray's opinions about aid to the Bolivian people. High Bolivian government officials began to offer Murray their friendship. A man of proven integrity, his reputation was that he could get things done. Friendships of earlier years were remembered as a new generation of public officials came into office. In all levels of Bolivian government, both Nova and Murray were received cordially with dignity and respect.

Murray felt honor bound to share his knowledge of Bolivia with his own country's representatives in order to assist in making more adequate use of foreign aid through his thorough understanding of the Bolivian mind. In the final period of his work in Bolivia, Murray shared the confidence of a large number of people in the governments of both Bolivia and the United States. He was interviewed by visiting dignitaries who sought opinions outside the embassy circles. He could be counted on for an honest appraisal colored only by his passionate desire to serve Bolivia with the greatest resources he could influence.

In a frank statement to Senator Wayne Morse during a breakfast session in La Paz in 1961, Murray set forth his philosophy clearly: "I believe that there are things which the government cannot do. Likewise there are things the church cannot do. They complement each other. Where the government must leave off in the field of ethical decisions, the church must pick up and teach people to make those decisions on how to use their resources. At the same time, the church must cease at the point where government can assume responsibility for providing materials and resources."

Political trends were more obvious to Murray than to most people. He disciplined himself to study Marxism and communism. He had recognized in Bolivia the tendencies to embrace philosophies intolerable to the Christian faith. The only way he knew to deal with such problems was to understand the opposing ideologies and strengthen his own convictions.

Murray Dickson ran the full gamut. He was fully dedicated as a missionary. Sacrifice of self and personal energy as well as resources was so commonplace that it was dismissed without second thought. His family, when called on to share this sacrifice, did so with enthusiasm, since it was "father's work and love." Murray was constantly concerned with the problems of his fellow workers. He could not judge others as less committed, but always sought practical solutions to the pressing problems of those who were under his supervision.

Convinced of the power of the church for good, Murray noted happily the subtle changes in governmental attitudes toward existing social conditions. During the 1960 session of the national houses of government in Bolivia, one third of the elected officials were graduates or former students of Methodist mission schools. Such representation gave Murray not only a means of communicating with government, but also cause for real hope in the future of Bolivia.

Murray saw change developing before people less astute imagined such a thing could be happening. He watched the colors of the scene while others were concerned with the movements of the figures. Mass media were always a part of Murray's consideration in directing the work of The Methodist Church in Bolivia toward increased service and extended ministries.

Education, medicine, and agriculture became major thrusts of The Methodist Church, with the traditional approach of the church being the golden thread binding the work together. Murray insisted that experts make decisions in each field. He sought technical help to provide the best solutions to specialized problems. He was quick to challenge friends in the states to donate their time and talents to specific projects.

Corruption, graft, bribery, cheating, and outright lack of respect for the law were prevalent throughout Bolivia when the Dicksons arrived in 1943; there was little difference in 1960 when Murray laid plans with his working partners for the following ten years. The one advantage and hope the workers shared was that Methodists were known as men of their word.

The world mission never escaped Murray in his involvement in Bolivia. He thrilled in response to reports of the World Council of Churches meeting in New Delhi, India, in 1961. His work was too confining to permit him to attend, but his spirit encompassed the world mission of the church. Once aware of the oriental groups living in crowded conditions in Hong Kong and Okinawa, his conviction grew that those people should be provided opportunity to use the jungles of eastern Bolivia to homestead. To this end he cultivated church groups which would sponsor such colonization. The areas had been tested and discovered to contain fertile soil and other desirable conditions.

Murray the farmer never lost his love for the soil. His interest, though disciplined to a fantastic task of immense human proportions, never lost sight of the basic hungers of men. He saw potential in areas others passed over ligthly because the problem permitted no easy solution. Practicality led Murray on many unrewarding chases, but when opportunity was provided to be helpful, Murray delighted in watching the progress of people whose lot he had bettered by some quiet, unsung effort.

Murray's life was mission; work was not just a job.

Living itself was a testimony to his love for God. From earliest teaching experience through years of extended responsibility, he never lost his joy of introducing new ideas. The most poverty-stricken farmer scratching in his limited plot of soil would listen in rapture as Murray described a new method to enhance another crop. Murray's spectrum was wide with experience and knowledge. His philosophy of life was made real and vital by a deep love of God. He found God in every human he met, in every scene he viewed, and in every thought he had.

One often told story of Murray's patience recounted a time when someone had been asked to do a little extra cleaning work. It went undone. The person was reminded. Murray discovered the work still undone and quietly cleaned, placing a fresh rose where the one who avoided the work would see it. A fresh rose and a thoroughly cleaned church confronted the person every time he entered it, until he finally realized the quiet way of love which Murray used to teach the humility of common tasks.

A tendency to think of Murray Dickson's life as ideal is quickly dispersed in reviewing the personal problems he encountered in physical discomfort, the pain of his family's sacrifices during his prolonged absences, near tragic illnesses, and his willingness to sacrifice himself for the comfort of others.

Not only was Murray's travel long and tedious, but much of it was dangerous. Delay after delay in his return at the appointed time created a philosophy of sacrifice in his family over the years.

Murray's horizons were unlimited. His visions were bright with plans he had for doing his Master's work. His constant objective was to portray the One whose name he implored in every task, whether joy or problem. With feet solidly set in the rocky terrain of the Bolivian mountains and in the vine-covered paths of the jungle, Murray struggled everyday to embody the love of Jesus Christ. He thrilled to the majesty of the mountains. He cried openly after seeing human misery, especially in little children. His capacity for love was infinite; his capacity for self-sacrifice was as large.

Murray Dickson knew the power of faith. If he sinned, it was in rejoicing in the victory of sacrifice.

A LAND
of
DECISION

In 1956 Bolivia was designated as a Land of Decision by the Methodist Board of Missions, thus crowning years of sacrificial effort. This action was confirmation of Murray's thesis since 1943; he saw unlimited potential if adequate resources and personnel could be obtained for the work.

Bishop Sante Uberto Barbieri, whose eloquence of spirit and insight were highly respected by church leaders, shared with Murray the credit for gaining Bolivia recognition as a major thrust of Methodist missions. Murray and Bishop Barbieri possessed a mutual affection, enabling them to work together in perfect harmony. Both men traveled extensively, and their moments together were potent with planning and decision.

As new support began to arrive in Bolivia, the work began to expand. Plans were laid, and new missionaries arrived on the scene. The dreams of missionaries for fifty years began to take visible form, but not without the continuing sacrifice of time and effort.

Expansion meant oversight and coordination. Murray accepted his responsibilities as executive director of The Methodist Church in Bolivia in the humility with which he approached every new task. His fellow workers knew they could depend on him, just as they could share the results of his endless and enthusiastic cultivation of the churches in the United States.

Travel became a taxing and constant necessity. Murray began to drive himself mercilessly during this period as his responsibilities increased. Problems with the constant change of altitude, bouts with insidious and disabling infections, and companionship with danger were no deterrent to Murray's efforts; he only drove himself harder. By 1956 his name was synonymous with Bolivia for many people.

Requests came from all levels of Bolivian leadership: "Please begin work in our area!" "Please get us a school!" "Please send your mission doctor to our area!" "Please provide help for our community to begin a cooperative!" The list grew longer, but Murray always listened patiently.

Murray was extremely conscious of the painful battle in which The Methodist Church had won the reputation of fulfilling its promises. He never gave a quick answer, but promised consideration of every request. Every petitioner could count on an answer which would set forth the conditions under which the church could answer his needs.

No one who approached Murray Dickson was ever abruptly dismissed. When he was not able to grant requests, he often suggested referral of the problem to another church or agency, including Roman Catholic groups when they were known to be especially proficient in the type of help needed. Many churches and groups drew from Murray's reservoir of knowledge.

No request was denied because of obvious problems or immediate difficulties; each was probed until a solution was found or the request proved impossible. Lack of funds was usually the culprit. It meant that Murray would drive himself harder to communicate with some friend or church who could provide the resources necessary to meet the growing requests made daily.

Murray Dickson and his co-workers made plans and dreamed with vision to provide the church with substantial guidelines for the expansion. The requests usually opened doors to areas previously considered in the planning. Murray's dreams and plans were recognized as logical progression for the church. These plans took shape during countless hours on the nearly impassable roads through mountains, across rivers, and in steaming, muddy jungles. Every flight was potentially an opportunity to work without interruption. Seldom was he fortunate enough to work without that interrution; nearly every flight he boarded in South America meant a reunion with a former student or friend.

In 1961 some three weeks before Murray's death, the author of his book accompanied Murray on a lengthy trip throughout western Latin America. In every airport Murray was hailed by some acquaintance and given the universal "abrazo" which indicated a warm and cordial friendship.

Murray was wanted everywhere at once. Each missionary had his pet project, inspired by the leadership Murray provided. Seldom was there a project without merit. Those who associated with Murray were very practical by nature, since they too shared the burden of providing the resources to achieve their dreams.

More personnel arriving on the field meant more problems to be dealt with. The common cry in face of seemingly insoluble problems was: "Wait until Murray comes!" And Murray always did come. He never allowed his personal concerns to enter into a decision about who needed him. This personal sacrifice was a direct result of love for a Master who held nothing back. To Murray Dickson to have held back anything someone needed, even if only his magnetic presence, would have belied the faith and love of his Master.

There were times when physical circumstances would not permit the usual planned approach. Such was the case in 1959 when Murray related the events of a very memorable trip he and Bishop Barbieri made to remote outposts. He wrote first of spending a day waiting for planes which could not take off and finally leaving before dawn the next day by jeep. He had promised the bishop nice weather with the rainy season past. His report continued:

> About kilometer sixty it began to rain. You remember how high the mountains, how narrow the roads, how slippery in wet weather. We crept along. Then there was the riverbed one drives up; there were rain, mud, and rocks working down it as we were working up it. It was past noon when we reached Aquile, the end of the rain, and a total lack of gasoline. Fortunately I had heard rumors of a gasoline strike and had ample.

> Later I felt a tire was low. . . . I decided to change. I discovered that the tire . . . was not my tire; it was worn completely through. . . . I am still trying to figure out who changed them. . . . We arrived at Sucre after driving twelve and one half hours. . . . There must have been fifty people there. . . . The bishop preached a thrilling forty-five minutes.

What a man! Afterwards people wanted to see me about getting married and other problems. I finally got to bed after ten, up at six in the morning after sleeping hard all night, though often when so tired I don't sleep like that. At seven there was another meeting. Then to get the car fixed (an exhaust pipe had broken off). Once the car was fixed, I began to try to get gasoline. The strike was on, and gas was not to be had anywhere, not even for five times the normal price. Finally I talked Point IV into lending me enough to get to Santa Cruz.

About nine o'clock I sensed the tire was low. . . . We were at about the highest point on the road to Sucre. There was . . . nothing to do but change the tire.

An epic struggle ensued. At last, with the tube out of the tire, Murray discovered that none of the patches would hold on the many holes. Using every ingenious method he could devise, he was still frustrated:

Finally at one A.M. I knew I was licked. There was no traffic on the road . . . nothing to do but walk. I figured it was thirty-two kilometers to Totora and bid farewell to the bishop, left him my poncho and what little coffee there was left in the thermos, and started out.

[With no moon to light the way over the treach-

erous roads, Murray walked the inside path next to
the mountains.]

At last I heard a little trickle of water off the
mountain and got a drink. Fortunately it was dark;
the next day, seeing it in daylight, I realized that I
wouldn't have dared drink of it if I could have
seen it.

Once I felt I could not go another step. . . . I lay
down on a big, flat rock beside the road, needing
desperately to sleep a little. . . . I slept for thirty
minutes, got up and struggled on. . . . My feet no
longer hurt; they were numb. My legs pained me
with every step. . . . When I was about to collapse,
I reached the foot of the hill over which one turns
down into Totora. It was only five o'clock, so I lay
down in a smooth spot of gravel beside the road.

Suddenly a horn sounded, and I lurched to my
feet, dazed, and struggled on. Again it sounded,
and then I realized that it was a donkey's bray! But
I was too cold to sleep and stumbled on up the hill.

[At dawn Murray entered the little town.]

A few people were up—Indians—but they couldn't
help me. It was almost seven when one of the
"hotels" opened up. I went in, asked for coffee, and
after fifteen or twenty minutes they brought me a
cup of black poisonous stuff, but the heat of it felt
good, and I gulped it down. They told me that
there was one evangelical in town . . . they didn't
know his name but would take me to his house.

The cobblestones brought my numb feet alive again
... and we stopped in front of an ancient, two-story
house. ... I knock and knocked. ... Finally a man
came out on the balcony. Who was it? The missionary leader who refused to let any of his young people have anything to do with the Methodists—the
man I told he was lacking in Christian charity in
showing such exclusiveness.

In this case Christian charity prevailed, and the couple
assisted Murray in returning to the vehicle with proper
tools, repairing the tire, and getting them on their way.

Once Murray and the bishop were making relatively
good time, they encountered landslides which further
delayed them. One incident amused the travelers: "At
kilometer 420 there was a chain across the road. This
is not a traffic-control post, so I got out to open the
chain. Two men came out and demanded what I was
doing. ... I asked them why the chain was there since
it was not a traffic stop. One of them laughed, 'Oh, the
chain bothers you, does it?' 'No,' I said, 'I think it is
funny.' I dropped the chain and drove quickly on, for
they were both very drunk."

A sleepless night and delays en route made Murray
extremely tired. To overcome the fatigue and to prevent
himself from going to sleep he asked the bishop to
question him constantly. They arrived in Santa Cruz

170

well behind schedule, only to discover that all travel had been forbidden. With unstable political conditions, all travel was uncertain. When news finally reached them that travel was permitted, Murray went immediately to obtain the necessary travel permits. Informed that special "passaportes locales" were necessary before the "hoja de ruta" (travel permission) could be issued, Murray and the bishop began the return trip to Cochabamba with neither. They passed the first barrier without incident and were delayed only by the usual landslides and vehicles stuck in fords in the river. Murray's impatience showed as he directed the rescue of an overloaded bus which could not make it out of the river ford onto the road:

> Nobody in the bus or in any of the cars or trucks waiting for it was doing anything. I found the driver and asked him about it. He said that the people wouldn't get off. . . . In a few minutes I had the people off the bus, a winch attached, and about twenty people helping push. We moved the bus a few feet, and someone said he heard a tractor coming, so we quit pushing and waited. . . . [In the comedy routine two more trucks managed to get stuck before Murray and the bishop were able to regain the road and continue.]

> Siberia was terrible, but we went on through [the perpetual rain forest] and were on the way down

171

the mountain toward Pojo when we rounded a corner and found a roadblock, a huge contingent of armed Indians. They searched the car rather thoroughly, though they were polite about it, and let us pass. About ten kilometers on there was another roadblock, but they were concentrating on a truck and waved us on. . . .

[During another delay at another landslide a friend recognized Murray and warned him to be extremely careful on the trip through the Cliza Valley where the night before a group of drunken Indians had murdered many persons with axes. It was disturbing news since the trip would be made late at night. The next roadblock proved the most thorough of the searches, leaving clothing, papers, and everything in a mess.] When they finished, they put two of their number in the back seat to accompany us. After we were moving, I looked back. Both of them, smelling heavily of coca, carried guns. I told the bishop they looked almost as scared of their guns as I was of them, but they really handled them as if they were accustomed to them and may have been more scared of my driving! . . . After fifteen minutes one of them tapped me on the shoulder and indicated in Quechua and universal gestures that I should stop. I did, and was relieved when he got out and walked away. Afterward the other repeated the performance, but as he got out, he said, "Bye, gracias." Where in the world do you suppose he got that "bye"? The bishop and I burst out laughing, perhaps as much from relief as from the ludicrousness of the situation. . . .

[Needing gas, Murray stopped at Montepunco, where he found a darkened station.] From a side room came maniacal laughter. We had to have gas. . . . After much cajoling, one of the three attendants, who were roaring drunk, came out to give us gasoline. We hurried on. I really feared the stretch through the Cliza Valley, but the moon was out, and the road was clear. Finally we approached the last traffic barrier near Cochabamba. . . . In recent months . . . [it] has been exceptionally strict. We had neither *hoja de ruta* nor *passaportes locales*. Two trucks had stopped, and they were being examined. The gate was open. The head official was attending the door of the shelter. I pulled slowly between him and the trucks, leaned out, and said, *"Buenas noches,"* and kept on going slowly ahead as if I had a right to. He did not whistle or call, so we went on into Cochabamba.

The next morning the bishop nearly missed his plane because of a wealth of misinformation and changes in flight plans caused by weather conditions. But he climbed aboard the plane while the motors were starting and promised to meet Murray for a trip on an equal basis to another part of the interior within a few days.

The Land of Decision was a country plagued by devisive factors of geography, tribal jealousies, and thoroughgoing distrust. Other letters Murray wrote amplified the dangers and unpredictable conditions of primitive travel. Schedules were often turned into complete folly.

Danger did not bother Murray, but any delays which prevented him from being more effective were intolerable. There was much to do, much to be seen and investigated as project after project materialized and communities waited for Murray's arrival to help them celebrate their accomplishment.

On the altiplano in the area around Lake Titicaca, where women were previously considered part of the economy of the farm and were never permitted an education lest they become dissatisfied with the menial life of a shepherdess, a school was opened for girls. The founding steps were taken for a vocational school to train boys in various trades.

In the cities it was a constant battle to train leadership to offer the masses not hollow preaching, but practical application of the mission to the whole man, which Murray saw as applying the love of his Master.

After the 1957 relocation of Okinawans and Japanese in the jungles not far from Methodist work in the Santa Cruz area, it became obvious that these people would affect the entire economy as a true asset. Their industry soon found them not only homesteading land according to their original grants, but also buying up the Bolivian homesteads and employing Bolivians by the hundreds.

Murray saw the need for someone to teach the children as well as for provision of a church for the Christians in the two colonies. Correspondence was initiated with the United Church in Japan. Did they have a missionary couple who would be willing to labor in the heat and problems of the Bolivian jungle with these Okinawan and Japanese people? Two years later Katsumi and Yoshee Yamahata arrived in Bolivia to begin their work.

Murray's profound international influence was evident. The Yamahatas, Japanese, served Japanese and Okinawans in remote eastern Bolivia, their salary paid by The Methodist Church in Switzerland, using work funds provided by The Methodist Church in the United States. Murray conquered a mountain of detail to provide a flourishing mission in the colonies.

Milestones in Methodist work were being passed with accelerated speed. Anniversaries were noted in a work that had reached adolescence. In 1957 the American Institute of La Paz, mother institution of all Bolivian Methodist work, celebrated its fiftieth anniversary. It was a totally different school from that which had struggled and nearly been lost in the mid-1940's.

It had grown, gained stature and respect. Murray was appointed director of the school for 1957, replacing Mario Salazar, who was in the United States as a crusade scholar.

The Bolivian government in recognition of the birthday decorated the school with the country's highest honor, the Condor of the Andes. Rather than accept the medal on his own lapel in behalf of the school, when asked to step forward, Murray turned to the school flag and asked the president to pin the decoration on the banner of the school. Murray's continual efforts at retiring from places of honor and pushing others into the foreground won him the undying devotion of many Bolivians and of his own colleagues.

With the growth of the Methodist work, the number of missionaries, and the constant demand for increased services in education, medicine, and agriculture, Murray's appointment as executive secretary of The Methodist Church in Bolivia had been natural. He had truly become "Mr. Methodist" of Bolivia by popular acclaim as well as the investment of himself in the ever-growing work.

Plans and dreams were his faithful companions on every trip as constantly increasing travel took him away from family and home. He consistently sought to perfect existing work. On a trip, if he were not driving but could yield the strain of fighting the wheel on rough Bolivian roads, Murray could frequently be caught with a faraway look in his eye. Seeing that look, one could be sure there was a new plan forming, a vision taking shape in details to which he would attend the first time he found a place steady enough so that he could write.

In spite of the scope of his work and the heavy demands upon him, he never lost his personal concern for his missionary co-workers or for the men, women, and children his mission served. He was personal. He was vitally interested and had the ability to make each successive person think he was the most important person in the world for the brief moment Murray Dickson spoke with him. Murray radiated the personal concern he had discovered during hours spent in the presence of his Master.

The Land of Decision meant Murray was faced with the constant task of making decisions; only history would show the wisdom and vision he exercised in those decisions. For Murray the battle for Bolivia was a personal fight against everything that stood in the way of his church assuming the position of servant among people who needed her services and her faith. An impelling urgency projected Murray as his big feet covered the rough terrain of the Land of Decision.

THE VOICE
of
MISSIONS

For Murray, 1959 and 1960 were years of travel, both within Bolivia and throughout the western hemisphere, representing The Methodist Church in Latin American missions.

The General Conference of The Methodist Church met in Denver in April of 1960. With some degree of hesitation Murray agreed to make a major portion of the report of the Board of Missions' World Division. He accepted the honor as a personal mandate to pour heart and soul into a convincing call to all Methodism to be more generous to her missions.

The Bolivian missionary staff had produced a special issue of *Highland Echoes,* the organ of Methodism in Bolivia. As usual this work had been entrusted to others with the request that a good issue be printed to carry to Denver representing Bolivia's accomplishments as well as needs. Not until after his presentation of the cause of missions in the General Conference did Murray realize what his fellow missionaries had done.

His embarrassment was obvious when he found that a tribute to his leadership was central among front-page articles in the issue he had distributed. The 5,000 copies spread the story of Methodism in Bolivia and included an analysis Murray had written of the history and prospects of Bolivian Methodism. Many leaders of The Methodist Church were confronted by the story of Bolivia for the first time. Because of Murray's warmth and enthusiasm, world missions gained new impetus. Murray was recognized among leaders of The Methodist Church as the "Voice of Missions."

Many experiences during years of sacrificial work combined in a spirit able to make missions live through story and illustration. Murray knew the people of the mission field. He had eaten with them; often it was not what he wanted to eat, and he had had to swallow hard. On one occasion during a very important visit to a local official deep in the interior, Murray saw maggots crawling in the meat he had been served. His host's meat was similar. As his host began to eat, Murray gulped and began to eat. Frequently he had no idea what beverages he was served in remote areas; perhaps this accounts for his bouts with dysentery and other intestinal disorders. Still he could not afford to offend his hosts if he were to manage a mutually acceptable agreement for new work.

Murray shared primitive sleeping conditions with the people. His beloved poncho wrapped around him, he put in many a night in flea-infested surroundings, seeking the first opportunity the next day to swab his bites with alcohol. Murray knew the hardships, dangers, and thirsts of the people from being with them and living as they did.

One night Murray might sweat in the heat and humidity of the jungle, the next he might shiver in the cold of the altiplano's frigid air. Jungle homes offered little but a thatched roof overhead. The altiplano hut became a collective shelter for animals and humans alike. The entire family, newborn lambs, litters of pigs, dogs, cats, and other animals were counted on for lending warmth. It was a long way from clean sheets and warm blankets; but it was all the people could offer, and Murray accepted in the spirit it was offered. In a hammock or on hard, cold, dirt floors, Murray went to sleep thinking how he could manage to help improve the conditions in which his hosts lived every day.

Murray knew politics. An avid reader, he read local papers wherever he found himself and sounded out local leadership on specific issues. He asked questions in such a way as to learn subtly the information not normally volunteered. Murray had the knack of making people feel his genuine interest in their opinions. Many found themselves telling him things they had not intended anyone to know. This enabled him to put his finger on the pulse of the country where he worked and to discover the thinking of a continent.

Murray Dickson saw the big picture. While concerned with details, he had the ability to discern movement and trends on national and international levels. Intensely interested in local conditions, he never let the immediate necessities of his work dull his view of the eventual outcome and need.

Murray was convinced of the power of God which is granted to His servants. Humility was his constant companion, but it did not dim his knowledge that God's guidance was a must if God's work was to be done. Persons who differed with him often came away with the feeling that they had gone against divine will when they dared to oppose Murray. Still he never lorded his authority over his associates, but sought their insights and opinions to produce the best decisions.

Two weeks after the General Conference in Denver, the Brazilian Methodist Church, an autonomous branch of Methodism, held its General Conference in São Paulo. Murray had been elected as fraternal delegate from the Bolivian Methodist Church.

The two weeks before leaving the United States were among the most fateful of his life. He had scheduled a number of appearances in large churches in Texas; among these were successive nights in Wichita Falls and Dallas. A group of old friends gathered around Murray after his presentation in Wichita Falls. They were driving to Dallas; would he care to accompany them? The answer was instant: he would, and together they would relive some of the old days at S.M.U. Somehow very little of the old days entered into the conversation.

All in the car were captivated by Murray's conviction that the future of The Methodist Church held the key to much of the future of Latin America. The men were leaders able to understand the importance of Murray's verbal picture of Latin American potentials. Lofty ideas fell on eagerly sensitive ears.

In the car that night were Dr. William H. Dickinson, pastor of Highland Park Methodist Church in Dallas—Methodism's largest congregation—and Dr. Donald Redmond, director of the Advance Specials Department of the Board of Missions. All these men shared friendships of long standing. Their conversation turned to the Bolivian Methodist Church and missions. A review of the history of inadequate support for the mission field drew a single stunning question from Dr. Dickinson. "Murray," he asked in a measured and thoughtfully provocative attitude, "what would it take to do the job in Bolivia now? I mean the whole job, not just a halfway job, but a substantial job to accomplish immediate objectives to help us realize the potentials you have spelled out for us?"

Murray could not believe his ears. As a leader, as a dreamer, he had considered the time when someone would ask that question, and he had thought many times of how he would answer. Suddenly the question had been asked. How would he answer it? It was then that the practical side of Murray Dickson answered with quiet confidence, "I am not sure, but I could tell you exactly and specifically within a few weeks."

As the traveling companions parted, they were promised a detailed schedule and cost estimate for such a substantial effort on behalf of missions in Bolivia. The seed was planted.

The dream began to take shape with practical applications. Medical centers, agricultural stations, additional technical personnel, specialists in education to develop leaders as well as educators, sociologists to study and recommend methods for modifying customs, public health workers—all received the careful attention of Murray's detailed plan as he penciled it. There was also coordination to be carried out with the foreign-aid sections of the U. S. government to avoid duplication of effort. It was a monumental dream, a staggering task.

In response to the question, "What would it take?" Murray sought to provide an answer. Some of the plans, many of the specifics in incomplete form, were in an unmarked folder in his desk. Ever so lightly penciled on the tab was "Dream!"

In a cloud of planning, Murray boarded the plane for Brazil. His thoughts were as high as the clouds above which he flew as he crossed the green carpet of unmarked Amazon jungle. The man whose comprehension of the work of the church was so inclusive arrived in São Paulo to add to his vast store of knowledge.

Mastering the subtle differences between Portuguese and Spanish during the conference, Murray was invited to preach in Central Church of São Paulo. He was impressed with the sprawling, struggling city of three million. He characterized the city for a friend as a parallel to the vivid Carl Sandburg portrait of Chicago. He observed the city which had grown too fast and which had deep-rooted problems in accommodating all the people who had flocked there in search of a brighter life. As usual Murray made an impact on the congregation with his sincerity and warmth.

Long-range plans for Latin America from the Board

of Missions made the Brazilian General Conference a natural time to unfold the news of a consultation on Latin American Methodism. This consultation would represent every country in Central and South America. Dates were set. Buenos Aires was to be the site. Murray was selected as coordinator; to him would be left the arrangements of the many details needed to make such a conference successful.

The consultation was a necessity. The Methodist Church faced varied challenges. There was much to be shared by which everyone could mutually profit. Other continental consultations had proved invaluable. Everyone thrilled at the prospect, but no one was more thrilled or more awed than Murray Dickson.

Leaving Brazil, Murray carried a second great dream, one demanding an immediate investment of attention. The first dream—an adequately supported program in Bolivia—was to receive only fleeting attention as planning for the consultation assumed priority.

Had it only been these two great ideas, along with the regular Bolivian work which demanded Murray's attention, one might understand the superhuman tasks to which Murray applied himself. Yet still another concern loomed on the immediate horizon.

No Protestant work in Ecuador had ever before become significant; a new united Protestant effort was projected. Almost without hesitation Murray was named as the Bolivian and Methodist representative for the venture. Sites were to be selected in which to begin work. Officials were to be cultivated and governmental guarantees sought. A subtle invitation had been expressed by the Ecuadorian government in several ways. Nothing was official, but the implication was strong enough to lead the churchmen to believe that the government would welcome Protestant work in Ecuador.

So began a series of trips which Murray made to the various points in Ecuador where members of the committee labored firmly to initiate work in the country. His last trip left him excited over the beginnings. It also left him physically exhausted as he prepared for a fast round of visits to mission outposts in his beloved Bolivia.

Murray's ability to grasp the scope of plans well into the future, along with his practicality, made him a valuable member of all groups of which he was a part. It is no wonder that his voice was recognized as a voice of missions representing The Methodist Church. His leadership and unusual ability were not overlooked. Here was a man with a grasp of missions who could not be wasted in detail work in some remote field, but who was a valuable tool in moving the total church to support missions programs which The Methodist Church desperately needed.

In October, 1960, Murray wrote to his father summarizing conversations with officials of the World Division of the Board of Missions. He had tried to laugh off the suggestions of various offers which might tempt him to leave the mission field for greener pastures. Murray was humbly complimented, but his first love was Bolivia. Had such conversations been known among leaders of the Bolivian Methodist Church, there would have been much anxiety.

In spite of his increased work load, Murray was only a little more difficult to see. And when one did manage to get him alone, there was the same warmth which had always prevailed when one spoke to Murray of personal concerns. A perfect understanding radiated from him in intimate conversation. This went with a confidence that made most problems seem simple to overcome if one only used Murray's capacity to believe.

The Central Conference of The Methodist Church, which included Argentina, Bolivia, Chile, Peru, and Uruguay, was held in Santiago, Chile, in 1960. The better-informed delegates from Bolivia sighed with relief when B. Foster Stockwell, head of Union Theological Seminary in Buenos Aires, was elected bishop. Murray's name had been prominent in balloting, but he had spent his time talking in behalf of Dr. Stockwell. One could not fail to miss the evident fact that it was only a matter of time until Murray would be considered for election as a bishop of The Methodist Church in Latin America. It was natural. Murray was respected as a leader throughout Latin America. In actual practice he had become the "Voice of Missions."

A NEW WORK
and a
COMMON CONCERN

The return to Bolivia after a year of extensive travel representing the country was welcome. It had been a furlough year for the family, but there had been little rest for Murray. Frances, the elder daughter, had entered Southwestern University at Georgetown, Texas.

Murray yielded to the pressures of proximity for government negotiations and left the beloved Cochabamba Valley to live in the capital city of La Paz. Travel was easier from La Paz, especially considering the many necessary trips to Ecuador and for the consultation in Argentina. Ease of travel, however, meant that he would spend less time at home. Nova and the

---

To this point the story of Murray Dickson has been told from research with the help of friends. I have been morally obligated to tell it. The remainder of the story is written from memory and my personal notes as I entered the picture and shared in the events. If there are errors, I trust they will be forgiven. Of necessity the first-person form of reporting is used, since I experienced the unbelievable period while serving as pastor of La Paz Community Church, the English-language congregation.

children would be surrounded by friends, but Murray would be away more than he was home.

The house he rented was less than a block from the university, so that student demonstrations usually resulted in their home's being filled with tear gas. The danger was not great, but the inconvenience was considerable. Close to the American Institute, Nova could teach a few classes in English and religion. Detailed negotiations with the Bolivian government demanded Murray's attention. The work expanded. Several new missionary families needed counsel in settling into their work. New work needed supervision. Cries were heard to begin more work.

The Methodist Church in Bolivia gained a reputation which was both enviable and distressing. It was enviable because it opened doors as Bolivians themselves requested help. It was distressing since the support was not sufficient to answer all the honest and worthwhile requests.

Murray began to use mission personnel to drive for him so he could spend time thinking. Every flight was a chance to work. Every night was a time to work in quiet when others had retired. Ecuador, the consultation, New York, new work, securing customs liberations for badly needed equipment and supplies, and a burning need to be a part of his favored Bolivian work drove him incessantly. He gave in to fatigue only occasionally.

October, 1961, saw Murray take several fast trips outside Bolivia. Exterior signs of fatigue were obvious to those close to him, but he would not slow down. The pressure of things to be done, the vision of what lay ahead drove him constantly on behalf of that to which he was committed. Then one morning he just could not get up. Dr. Louis Tatom was summoned. A shot or two, a brief two days in bed during which he slept most of the time, and Murray was on his way again. The brief confinement only served to double his intensity of commitment. From the two days in bed came a resolution to make every trip and every hour pay double dividend.

Murray Dickson walked with a purpose. Seldom did anyone ever see him strolling along. Even with no outward pressure, the habit was so great that there were a long, purposeful stride and a quick pace to his walk. To walk more than three blocks with Murray was an exhausting experience, especially if he were in a hurry. Long legs stretched out, and the big feet covered ground resolutely.

Many ideas were constantly stirring in Murray's mind in late 1961. Allowing himself the luxury of a few minutes to put his private thoughts into words, Murray

191

captivated close friends with his view of the importance of the impending consultation of Methodist churches in Latin America. His pile of correspondence grew. His enthusiasm multiplied for the work of properly overseeing the conference in its last minute detail to assure the greatest possible profit.

During a conversation Murray confided to me that the pressure was growing. He needed help. Would I be willing to travel with him and help where I could on a trip to Buenos Aires? It did not take a second invitation.

A few days later as we left La Paz, I sensed that Murray was relieved to have company. He was tired; how tired I did not realize until we were aboard the plane. Murray slept for most of the trip. It was not a light doze, but the profound sleep of the exhausted. At each stop people waited for him with work. Cochabamba was the first stop. The forty-five minute sleep had restored his energy. A delayed flight was welcomed as an opportunity to work further with those who treasured the few extra minutes they were permitted with Murray.

Flying to Santa Cruz, Murray slept again. Due to the delay in Cochabamba, the time on the ground in Santa Cruz was reduced severely. Going on to attend to baggage and save seats, I feared Murray might not make it aboard the plane. He waited until the last possible second before boarding. It was business till the last minute.

Once again Murray slept deeply for several hours. Then with Buenos Aires only a short flight ahead, he wakened, fresh, alert, and thoroughly companionable as he shared a wealth of stories about his previous trips over the same route by air and surface.

Here Murray Dickson was at his delightful best. All else was shut out but his concentration on making past experiences live. A master storyteller, he left out no detail which would make the story glow in vividly colored word pictures.

Not long before we reached Buenos Aires, Murray began to open his personal life to review. Quickly I realized that I was hearing what few persons had ever heard. Some of the story pertained to the delight of the days ahead, some indicated his pride in his family, some drew verbally a picture of the work of The Methodist Church in Bolivia and throughout South America, and some expressed concern over the decisions which lay immediately before him.

There was almost a compulsion within him to share his ideas. Not until many days later did I recognize the reasons for his urgent relevance in sharing those ideas. It was more than an intuition of foreboding. His mind was full of what lay ahead. He thrilled and caused me to thrill to the hopes he spelled out vividly. It was as if he were compelled to open his whole mind and spill out his thoughts.

In Buenos Aires I had to run to keep up. Murray took time to point out the most interesting parts of the city, relating stories and statistics about the great city on the Rio de la Plata. He included an analysis of current political situations. His commentary was proved right the morning after we arrived, when we were warned to be cautious in venturing from the hotel. A general strike and a fight had been staged the night before. We saw vivid evidence of the clash in gutters which, although being flushed, still ran red with blood.

Murray never overlooked such indications of the adolescence of Latin America. Inwardly disturbed, he accepted the evidence of man's violence against man as a call to throw everything in his being into the fight for right by love and persuasion.

On the second day we made our headquarters at Union Theological Seminary. His first appearance caused the usual stir which occurred wherever Murray Dickson went. There were numerous old friends to be greeted with a pertinent personal question to each about study, family, or church. Murray was the center of festive reunions. I marveled at his sphere of influence and the respect he commanded.

Meetings consumed several days. After each meeting, Murray would return to the room where he had left me with a stack of typing or other work, and we would start out on a fast trot to stretch our legs.

The general strike caused a severe shortage of the famed Argentine beef. We had to settle for delicious shrimp and other local dishes. Chagrined, Murray promised that we would get good beef before we left Buenos Aires, and we did.

Murray was invited to preach on Sunday morning in Central Methodist Church, where large and very attentive congregations heard his sermons. Following each service, he was besieged by people who wanted to renew friendships or identify themselves to this articulate representative of The Methodist Church in Bolivia. The hope toward which he worked was evident in his preaching. His affirmation of faith in the universal church was powerful and moving in sermons that morning. Nearly an hour after the last service, Murray was finally free to accept a luncheon invitation.

The Buenos Aires trip was not all work and dullness. Murray's humor made all work and travel into adventure. Perhaps the most embarrassing experience of Murray's life occurred when we ventured into a smart

shop in a suburb of Buenos Aires to look for the bathing suit he had promised his younger daughter, Margaret. Shown a wide variety of suits, he selected one he
liked.

"What size, Señor?"

"Well, it is for my daughter, you know. She is
fifteen."

"But, Señor, what size is she?"

"About usual for her age."

The salesgirl disappeared. She returned with several
girls, all attractive and in varying sizes and shapes. As
the models lined up, the clerk asked Murray to indicate
the one whose figure best represented that of his
daughter.

Murray turned several shades of pink and appealed to
me for help. Standing to advantageously display their
figures, the girls drew their hands down across busts
and hips and inquired in falsely seductive tones, "Is
she my size, Señor?" Murray was beside himself. Sensing his discomfort and obviously believing that the
swimsuit was for someone other than a daughter, the
girls added to his plight by rapid-fire, suggestive questions.

Margaret nearly missed getting a bathing suit. Had
Murray not promised her one, I am certain that we
would have fled the shop in a flash. At last Murray

settled on a girl whose figure fitted the disturbed memory of his daughter, and the purchase was completed. We left the shop in a chorus of hilarity and devilish laughter of young ladies who had thoroughly enjoyed Murray's discomfort and embarrassment.

Flying across the River Plata on a quick trip to Montevideo, Murray spoke to a number of Uruguayans, among whom was Mortimer Arias. Murray had confided that part of his mission on the trip was to persuade Mortimer to go to Bolivia to work. He was successful. Several months later Mortimer and his family arrived in Cochabamba. Another trip had done double-duty.

On the flight back to Bolivia Murray was in an expansive mood; all kinds of subjects were discussed. There was little sleep on this trip. There were the expected delays, and as usual we never stopped at an airport without Murray's being greeted by some old friend or acquaintance.

Murray had spoken of long-range plans and needs for the church. Not knowing of his commitment to the Texas group to provide a plan for the acceleration of the work of Methodism in Bolivia, I found myself a party to discussions on what I would do were I given a free hand and adequate resources. Murray's questions were provocative and penetrating. We came to conclusions which I later realized would have been a part of his plan had Murray lived to carry it out.

Confiding that he had held extensive conversations with officials of the Board of Missions about improving communications between the field and the local church, Murray struck a nerve vital to me. We explored the possibilities extensively.

About the time we were called for reboarding in Salta, a capital city in northern Argentina, set in a little, cuplike valley surrounded by mountains, we were entering discussions about our hopes and dreams for our future personal work. Carefully Murray worked the conversation around to the place where, without knowing the implication, I agreed to spend some time working on a plan to improve the communications between mission field and the local church. Murray was thinking well ahead of me and leading me in a direction which had already taken shape in his future plans. I was committed, but I did not discover how deeply until several weeks later when I visited the offices of the Board of Missions to relate details of Murray's death.

Suddenly on takeoff we sensed problems with the aircraft. Tense moments followed until the pilot managed to keep the limping plane from hitting the mountain wall ringing the airport and brought it to a safe

emergency landing. Once on the ground, a silence overcame us. Then spontaneously came the most profound
sharing of faith and philosophy of life I have ever
known. This had not been Murray's first experience of
danger in the air. Danger was his constant companion.
This instance only provoked a renewed response. Was
it premonition? The narrow escape had made us both
confessional. We spoke openly about our plans for
families in event of death. We spoke of our faith for
what lay ahead and the unknown qualities of life. The
conversation was not morbid, but thoroughly refresh-
ing. Little did I realize that several sentences from
that conversation would stand out in my mind when I
confirmed to Murray's wife the tragic news of his
death.

As we neared Bolivia, our conversation became more
intense and rapid. There was much to be said, so little
time to say it. Murray's deepest problems were evident.
Difficult decisions lay immediately before him. He
acknowledged that his course would be determined
during the consultation and in the Central Conference
meeting in special sessions following the consultation.

Bishop Stockwell, elected only a few months previously, had died suddenly. During his election Bolivian
Methodists had been disturbed by the popularity Murray had shown in the balloting. They feared losing him

to the ranks of the episcopacy. Following Bishop Stock-well's death, Bolivians often mentioned Murray as a logical successor. Murray's personal reaction was typical. Those who knew him well were not surprised to hear him say he was not good enough. Murray measured himself by Bishop Barbieri and others he had known, loved, and respected. It was the stance he had used before in arguing that he was not good enough for the ministry. Others thought differently. Murray was complimented, but deeply disturbed. It seriously colored his decisions.

Expressing these confidences required no request for secrecy. The rapport was profound. We had shared deeply of our convictions and our concerns. Within three weeks I would discover the full implication of the portions of the story which Murray did not tell. I would also discover that he had persuaded me to commit myself to a work in which we both had great interest, but which neither of us would be permitted to try.

As we left the plane in La Paz, I noticed that Murray was weary. The fatigue lasted only a moment. The sight of his wife and children sparked him to new energy, and to all outward appearances he was refreshed and ready to begin work.

Another trip, another opportunity had worked triple-duty on behalf of the church he loved. The completed journey had been south, and in a few days another would take him north on behalf of the new work in Ecuador.

Work met Murray wherever he traveled. People and their problems filled hours of precious time. None was ever turned away without his personal counsel. When anyone hurt, Murray hurt. When anyone was concerned, Murray managed to shoulder some of the anxiety. This was his life. It was a constant attempt to bring the love of his Master into the lives of those with whom he worked and to whom he ministered as pastor and administrator.

THE LAST TRIP
for the
BIG BOOTS

It would be an almost free evening. Murray could complete his interviews by 8:30 P.M., and we could enjoy a rare diversion from our routines. Sidney and Lou Tatom would go along. Nova and my wife, Ellen, would complete the sixsome for a good meal and a quiet evening spent enjoying such compatible company.

The food was exceptionally good and the company in rare humor that mid-December Thursday evening of 1961. Murray's relating of some of the more humorous events of the Buenos Aires trip and his repertoire of stories made the evening a joy.

Friday was a heavy day of work for everyone. Plans were changed for a trip to Caranavi. Word had reached La Paz that Enrique Chiccetti, the Argentine doctor working in the mission station at Caranavi was ill. I was to have driven for Murray, but instead he and Lou Tatom arranged to leave as early on Saturday morning as they could get everything together.

The usual number of problems remained to be solved, people to be seen, and details to be attended to before Murray jumped into the Volkswagon driven by Dr. Tatom. As they rolled down the hill, I waved to them, and Murray gave me a letter to mail which he had typed in the early-morning hours. It was to his father, containing expressions of affection and concern over his parents' health. With a hearty laugh, they were off.

Sometime later, I was in a warm bath enjoying the unusual combination of water and electricity at the same time, when the phone rang. It was Nova. Her words were short: "Jim, come please. There has been an accident!" At Nova's words I felt a surge of dread. A few minutes later I stood in Nova's bedroom and heard the unbelievable story. Murray and Lou had been in an accident. Details were agonizingly incomplete. The railroad had relayed the information that Dr. Tatom was seriously injured and Murray also badly hurt. Both were being sent on the little railroad which wound up through the mountains from 3,500 feet to the "cumbre" (crest) at 16,000 feet and then back down into La Paz. The trip from La Paz to the cumbre was at best an hour's hard drive. Perhaps we could intercept the train there.

Dr. Bill Jack Marshall at the Methodist hospital had been alerted. We decided that we should head for the cumbre as quickly as I could pick him up. Faster than ever before I made the trip to the clinic where Dr. Marshall waited with considerable medical equipment, including cots and oxygen. Wasting no time, we loaded the equipment and began our fight with time to beat the train to the cumbre.

We drove as fast as the carryall would move. At the outskirts of the city, at the traffic-control point, the gate was up, and we roared through without slackening speed. We needed all the momentum we could muster to make the climb. Behind us, trailing as closely as they dared, were Mario Salazar and his brother Noel. Safety was no factor. We were driven by a haunting fear of what we might find.

The little stone station on the cloud-shrouded mountain sheltered three employees. Our questions brought little information, but what we heard there was final: Dr. Tatom had died in the crash, and his body was due in the station in an hour.

It was thought that Murray was still alive and would arrive at the cumbre in a few minutes. Again we jumped into the carryall to attempt to intercept the truck in which Murray was riding and thus gain a few precious minutes in rendering treatment. We had hardly begun to move when we met a series of trucks; The second carried Murray's body. Instantly Dr. Marshall was out of our vehicle and on top of the truck where Murray's warm, still body was covered by blankets. He had not been dead more than a few minutes. Questions posed to the truck driver concluded the tragic news. Dr. Tatom was indeed dead, and his body was on the train due, as we had been told, in about an hour.

Emptiness—despair—grief—and many other emotions consumed us as we stood on the cold, foggy road at 16,000 feet. It was a bad dream. It could not be true. Yet in the back of my vehicle was the lifeless body of one who had been so warm, so alive, so vital a few hours before.

Three months later we managed to piece the story together. Wearing his poncho and big boots, Murray had traveled with Lou into the foggy area of the mountain pass. Slowly they wound their way down the twisting cutbacks and steep-straight portions of the road to Unduavi. Duly registering at the traffic control, they climbed out of Unduavi toward Coroico. The fog was thicker as they literally drove in the clouds. As they rounded a very sharp curve at kilometer 51, they met a truck with lumber fresh from the valley. The long overhang brushed the light station wagon as it perched precariously on the outside edge of the road. One wheel dropped off the road, and a second later the vehicle tumbled to the railroad right-of-way hundreds of feet below.

As the story unfolded later from a former student of Murray's who was on a truck following the lumber truck, Murray either survived the impact or else managed to get out of the vehicle before it hit the tracks. Suffering a deep gash on his forehead, Murray managed to climb partway back up the hill, where a rope was thrown to him by people who had stopped. By this time, however, he was so weak that within a few feet of the road he collapsed and fell down the rock face of the mountain once more. The group then went by road down to a place where they could recover the bodies of the two men by walking along the railroad tracks. They took Murray, still alive, to Unduavi, but the only medical attention available was in La Paz.

Several months following the accident I was approached by a man who asked if I had heard the whole story of the accident. He indicated that he was the owner of a fleet of trucks. Sometime after the fatal crash one of his regular drivers was arrested and jailed on a drunken-driving charge. Using their usual methods to obtain confessions, the police had beaten the man until he was delirious. At that point the truck owner was called to the jail. He heard his driver repeating a remorseful story about the horrible thing he had done at kilometer 51. When capable of answering questions, the driver poured out the story of knocking the Volkswagon off the road at the 51-kilometer mark. Nothing could be done, nothing proved. Irreversible tragedy was at least given explanation in more detail.

Our trip back to La Paz was slow and careful. Through a film of tears we saw little until we arrived at Nova's home and walked into a room filled with people. As we entered, a hush fell over the assembled group. Nova looked up and said with a smile, "It's okay, fellows, I think I know." In a more private setting we reported what little we knew.

Nova's reactions were amazing. She had lived in dread of such news for years yet her only question was, "Shouldn't we bury him here in Bolivia?" My answer reflected the ideas Murray shared on the trip from Buenos Aires. It was all Nova needed to hear. Her decision was made easier in the thought that it was Murray's wish. She then ordered us to go to be with Sidney Tatom and return to arrange funeral details later.

A frenzy of activity occupied everyone. Anyone who could lose himself in pursuit of some detail, no matter how trivial, did so. Surely the whole thing was a bad dream. Then as we copied what Nova dictated for the cables to be dispatched to family and friends, the stark reality of the tragedy hit us.

The cables to the states were delayed and misrelayed. The few which did get through were misinterpreted by those who received them. Nova had dictated, "Murray died today in a mountain pass"; friends thought the death was due to a heart attack or natural causes. The Board of Missions would know nothing of the death of Dr. Tatom until I called on the following Tuesday morning from Miami International Airport, where I was awaiting a flight to take Mrs. Tatom and the girls to Gainesville, Florida, to bury Dr. Tatom.

There remained only a few tender offices we could render. The trip down the hill to the American clinic was slow and tragically sad. The bruised and lifeless body lay in the back of my carryall. When we arrived at the clinic, loving hands relieved us of the sacred burden and began making the necessary preparations.

Questions flooded our searching minds. Could fatigue and the complications of a recent cold have been a contributing factor in Murray's death? Could we have done something more which would have saved his life? And the greatest question of all—why?

My last view of the final stages of preparation that night was of Murray's inert body lying peacefully after it had been lovingly washed by nurses in the hospital where he had experienced so many happy moments in the births of his three children. At the end of the table lay the red poncho, stained with blood, and under the table were the big boots, tops folded over in a sad droop expressive of our feelings—what feelings were left in us.

In a matter of a few hours the world had turned cartwheels for several families. A whole church and a countless host of people were caught in the web of sorrow. The only comfort was the realization that no time could dim the memory of the warm, bright eyes and the enthusiastic personality which carried a message of hope.

Local laws were to be observed. Murray would be buried the following day—Sunday afternoon—December 17, 1961. An employee of the American clinic was dispatched to the market area where caskets were sold. His task was almost impossible: to find a casket large enough to accommodate the body which was head and shoulders taller than most Bolivians.

THEY DUG
HIS GRAVE
TOO SHORT

Sunday morning dawned brilliantly. The day before seemed like an exceptionally bad dream. No one had slept much. Even those using sleeping pills to seek the escape of slumber had passed through a haunted night. During the night people had responded to the evident needs. Everyone shared the loss. The Dickson family had lost a father and husband, but all Bolivia had lost a friend. The Tatoms in a short period of time had also endeared themselves to a community, and friends shared their simultaneous tragedy.

Before the funeral there were Sunday morning services to be conducted as usual. How could they be usual? My sermon, carefully prepared well in advance, was laid aside. A strange combination of emptiness and overwhelming compulsion to sound a reassuring note prodded me. All morning the telephone rang. Would the eleven-thirty service be held? "Yes," rang the answer with a note of triumph. What better time for a service!

The English-speaking community seemed to have suddenly grown. Mutual loss brought them together. The two men had left a host of friends. Hymns were sung with more conviction and thought than enthusiasm. Partway through the reading of the New Testament lesson, emotion caused me to contemplate calling the service off and retreating to a place where I could give in to the emotion and grief which I so keenly felt. There were others seeking some word of comfort—and all of us were seeking an answer. "Why?"

I will probably never again feel the concentrated petitions of a congregation in prayer and seeking as in that potent hour. More than rising to the occasion, this was living testimony to our faith. The hour climaxed with the singing of "A Mighty Fortress Is Our God." Then we sought lunch before attending the funeral.

Iglesia La Reforma (Church of the Reformation) had been built with funds received from One Great Hour of Sharing in 1955. Stately, spotlessly clean, and with the characteristic odor of floor wax, it was the setting for the funeral. Preparations were completed early. Long before three o'clock no room remained. People crowded into the sanctuary where a simple mahogany casket stood before the altar. Inside the chancel rail Indian women sat, some with babies on their backs. The ambassador to Bolivia from the United States, Ben Stefansky, upon arrival was given what preference could be afforded. He stood in the balcony among common Bolivians.

When Nova and the children arrived, a new note was sounded. She wore not the traditional black of mourning, but a tailored suit of brilliant blue. On her face was a confident smile, even though an occasional tear trickled down her cheek. On either side Margaret and George gave mutual support and found comfort in her strength.

The funeral was mercifully short. Tributes rang with the conviction of triumph in the Christian life. The three of us whose sad privilege it was to conduct the service used English, Spanish, and Aymara (a local Indian dialect). Though following no prearranged theme, those who understood all three men marveled that each said essentially the same thing. Life eternal was Murray Dickson's theme song. He lived in the reality of life eternal, and his death, for all its tragedy, was a translation to that toward which his entire life had always been directed. Handel's "I Know That My Redeemer Liveth" had the effect of a rousing marching song of victory. Worshipers at the funeral felt they had seen faith in perfect evidence.

As the pallbearers gently and reverently carried the casket from the church, a man who had been greatly helped and influenced by Murray could not stand it. He stepped out and found a spot where he could assist in carrying the earthly remains of his friend.

Outside a hearse was waiting. As the casket was being placed in it, a group of youth in a reverent mood edged their way forward. They took the casket, placed it on their shoulders, and carried Murray's body down the steep hill to the street known as El Prado. Carrying the casket was a final tribute indicating their love and respect for a man whose influence had touched each of their lives. Murray thus received a tribute reserved for only the most respected Bolivians.

It was a slow, agonizing procession. The strain was beginning to tell on Nova. Several of us at her side asked if we should step in and speed up the procession. "No," she quietly replied, "Murray belonged to them too, and this is something they must do." Up the main street of La Paz went the procession. There have been larger ones, but none with the silent, yet triumphant atmosphere of this one.

At the end of the usual route, the casket was placed in the hearse and the followers hurried up the hill to the Anglo-American Cemetery. As we entered the cemetery, a sudden thunderstorm broke and drenched everyone. It seemed that the heavens had opened and were pouring copious tears over our feeble efforts of final respect. In the midst of this downpour the committal was read in the three languages. Not a person moved or gave any indication of physical discomfort in the soaking rain. Every heart was intent on the last tender office taking place. Finally, in English, I concluded my prayer and looked across the open grave to see Nova tearful, but smiling.

The cemetery workers pushed through the crowd and with crude ropes and boards began to lower the casket. Then there were quiet, nearly frantic orders. We were surprised to see the casket hoisted and placed to one side of the grave. The grave was too short! During nearly twenty years of dealing with human inadequacies, inconsistencies, and the unpredictable circumstances of Bolivia, Murray had smiled through the problems. When it came time to place his mortal body in its resting-place, his grave was short!

Somehow the situation seemed eloquent testimony— no grave could hold the spirit of one whose footsteps had scaled the mountains, traversed the plains, and made paths in the valleys of his adopted country. As I looked at Nova, her rain-streaked face had broken from the reserved but confident smile, and she laughed heartily at this final incident in Murray's journey. If such incidents are observed in heaven, I am sure heaven rocked with the hearty laughter of Murray Dickson, who would have loved this ironic, concluding scene to his mission in Bolivia.

Little impressions stand out in memories burdened with the intensity of such emotions as we shared. When the casket was finally lowered, we felt the earth had received the body of one whose spirit would work in Bolivia long after the body was dust. As we left the cemetery, the lovely, high-walled setting, isolated in the midst of a bustling industrial section, seemed a hallowed and appropriate place.

It had been a strenuous afternoon. As I arrived at Nova's home following a change into dry clothing, I was met by Murray's son, George. His words expressed what all of us tried to say, yet never seemed to put into the correct words: "Gee, Uncle Jim, I sure am glad we are Christians."

OTHER
SHEEP
I HAVE

Murray Dickson had died with the boots on his big feet and the faded red poncho around his broad shoulders. One tribute paid in deepest reverence during the funeral recalled the words of Jesus in John's Gospel: "And I have other sheep, that are not of this fold; I must bring them also" (10:16 RSV). He lived and died serving others. The entire passage reflects the spirit of service and dedication to sacrificing himself for their redemption.

Murray left much unfinished business, but his example and memory spurred many others to achievements they had never dreamed of before. His spirit continued to move in and through people with whom he had worked and shared the vision of things to come.

Several great moments toward which he was working went unrealized. As important to him as the Latin American consultation toward which he was laboring was a baccalaureate address he was scheduled to deliver at Southwestern University in Georgtown, Texas, where his daughter Frances was studying. Southwestern lost its baccalaureate speaker. Instead Nova proudly accepted the posthumous award of an honorary doctor of divinity degree at the spring ceremonies. Murray's cycle was completed. The man who had felt that he was not good enough to be a minister was cited as an outstanding pastor. Schools, governments, and individuals all were insistent on recognizing Murray's great spirit.

In a joint session the two houses of government in Bolivia posthumously honored Murray Dickson with the highest decoration conferred by Bolivia, the Condor of the Andes. In the citation he was credited with having contributed greatly to the welfare of Bolivians through his efforts in education and leadership in The Methodist Church which provided assistance to Bolivia. The House of Representatives of the state of Texas and the United States Senate noted Murray's efforts as recorded in the *Congressional Record* of January 29, 1962 (pp. A633-34).

As the tributes continued to pour in to the family, the Board of Missions' headquarters in New York, and the Bolivian Methodist Church, new leadership stepped into the vacancies created by Murray's death. Jim Pace assumed responsibilities as executive secretary for The Methodist Church in Bolivia. After a year he returned to his first love, Wesley Seminary, where training ministers had been a task of cardinal importance to Murray. Paul McCleary stepped into the exectuive secretary post when he returned to the field following an abbreviated furlough. Both gave capable leadership in the tradition Murray had established.

Each person had a different way of saying that Murray had added dimension to his life. A spirit of awe and reverence was felt in each such attempt to put into words what so many acknowledged. In one such lovely tribute Wilson Boots, who had profited from Murray's guidance and moral support during his first term on the mission field, wrote to Murray's children:

> Nora and I have been wanting to write each of you to share our sense of gratitude to God for the life and witness of your father in our own lives and in the lives of a vast multitude of people. His life is one of the truly great ones in the world mission of the Christian church in the twentieth century, and we give thanks daily to the Father for his gifts to us all through Murray Dickson. We would not be serving here in Argentina had it not been for his work in the American Institute of Cochabamba. During our recent visit to Bolivia we had many opportunities to get together with Bolivians and share what your father's life means to the lives of many and what his continuing presence with us in

the spirit means to us individually and to the whole Bolivian church.

Wilson Boots put into words what many wanted to say and what all were quick to affirm. Murray would live in the lives of Bolivians and of all who knew him. His spirit would permeate the work of The Methodist Church in Bolivia for many years as his personal investment resulted in the dividends of new leadership. His plans were the foundations upon which a great new church would rise up for the living Christ.

Before leaving Bolivia for the United States with her children, Nova prepared a short statement in which she expressed appreciation for the many courtesies extended her during the time of tragedy. She referred to Murray's new appointment in the larger work of the Kingdom. In Spanish, the words, *el nuevo nombramiento* (the new appointment) meant a great deal to the Bolivian people, who were well aware of the spirit of Murray Dickson in all they attempted and would attempt in their church.

That spirit continued to be felt elsewhere also. Under the leadership of Dr. Donald Redmond of the Advance Department of the Methodist Board of Missions, Murray's folder marked "Dream" came out of the files and became the plan by which Methodism would commemorate the lives of Murray and Dr. Tatom. "Operation Murray Dickson" took its name in memorial of the two whose missions extended far beyond what anyone realized.

Bolivians also moved to extend the most profound recognition. The group having responsibility for the statue honoring outstanding Bolivian educators by-passed a long-standing rule that only native Bolivians could be so honored, and the name of Murray S. Dickson was placed immediately beneath the name of Dr. Angel Salazar, father of Bolivian Methodist leaders Mario, Noel, and Hernan Salazar. In this outwardly simple but profound way Murray was made a Bolivian. He had earned his place among Bolivians who were considered giants of education.

Operation Murray Dickson implemented the dreams Murray had sketched out. Its projects appealed to a large number of churches throughout the United States where Murray and Dr. Tatom were held in high esteem and had broadened the understanding of missions by their personal interpretation and involvement.

Number one on the list of priorities was the training of effective national leadership. It had been Murray's passion and haunting concern. A clergy trained only to serve the church was not the answer. The clergy and leadership of the mission field had to provide its own support, be able to teach subjects in addition to religion, and be able to serve in capacities of community development in whatever situation they were appointed for service. Wesley Seminary, geared to train such leadership, began to expand. Within a three-year period after Murray's death, the seminary's main building was completed and dedicated to Murray's memory. He had contributed significantly to the establishment of this institution of practical training immensely important in the future of Bolivian Methodism.

National leadership matured rapidly. From a handful of national pastors, poorly trained but enthusiastic, the trained leadership grew in 1967 to 38 conference members in full connection and 140 local preachers, along with an increasing number of teachers, administrators, and others whose training in Methodist institutions enabled them to serve the church. When the appointments were read at the conclusion of the 1967 Annual Conference, there were seven district superintendents, six of whom were Bolivian. The church had begun to fulfill Murray's dream of a well-trained and effective national leadership.

Gains and increases were seen in all facets of the work of The Methodist Church in the years following Murray's death. From two organized churches in the mid-1950's, the church grew to 48 fully organized congregations with more than 120 other preaching places on the way to being organized. By the end of 1967 there were more than 4,000 full members. (In the system of serving a year's probationary membership, this reflects a well-trained group willing to accept the duties of membership. Several hundred probationary members were reported at the Annual Conference of the Bolivian Methodist Church in 1967.) The local church was beginning to reach stages of real effectiveness.

As the frontier pushed deeper into the Amazon basin, the road on which Murray had suffered his fatal injuries became a major supply route for opening the Alto Beni area. Plans were projected to extend the road into the very heart of the Amazon, and construction began. The future development of oil and agriculture shows unlimited potential and opportunity. People follow the exploration teams and homestead as quickly as new roads are cut.

Bolivian economy changed. Discovery and production of oil, along with growing agricultural production of rice, sugar, cotton, timber, and other products enabled Bolivia to enter the world markets in commodities other than the traditional tin and ores. This produced revenue for new roads, improvement of existing roads, and the development of better air travel and communications. The political scene remained erratic.

Those who are cautiously optimistic today see evidence of the exercise of real democratic process emerging.

A new social concern and conscience developed first among the young leaders, then became evident throughout the whole church. Service became an opportunity rather than the drudgery of obligation as it had been previously regarded. Slowly men began to make practical application of the faith they embraced.

The Methodist Church had been instrumental in helping to produce a climate in which such things as a social conscience and a stable government could develop. Sixty years had seen the laying of solid foundations at a cost of heroic effort on the part of many. Murray Dickson's name is near the top of the list.

Murray's spirit continues to evidence its influence in Bolivia. His faith, expressed in a letter to a friend shortly before his death and illustrated by the way he lived, best explains the driving convictions still evident in the memories the people of Bolivia have of him: "One of the glorious things about eternal life is that it begins the moment it is chosen. This is the source of the Christian's faith, hope, and security. For the real Christian does not have to accept blindly an abstract and hypothetical doctrine of eternal life—he can experience it, taste a little of it, know something of it here and now. Indeed, a person is not really Christian unless he is already living in eternal life."

Just as the big boots left indelible prints in the soil of the mountains, jungles, and valleys of Bolivia, Murray's spirit left permanent marks in the lives of the people and church of Bolivia.